JUNGLE DOCTOR
Meets a Lion

⑨

JUNGLE DOCTOR
Meets a Lion

Paul White

CF4·K

10 9 8 7 6 5 4 3 2 1

Jungle Doctor Meets a Lion ISBN 978-1-84550-392-5
© Copyright 1950 Paul White
First published 1950, reprinted 1951, 1952
by Paul White Productions,
4/1-5 Busaco Road, Marsfield, NSW 2122, Australia

Published in 2008 by Christian Focus Publications, Geanies House,
Fearn, Tain, Ross-shire, IV20 1TW, Scotland, U.K.
Fact files: © Copyright Christian Focus Publications

Cover design: Daniel van Straaten
Cover illustration: Craig Howarth
Interior illustrations: Boothroyd
Printed and bound in Denmark by Norhaven A/S

Since the Jungle Doctor books were first published there have been a number of Jungle Doctors working in Mvumi Hospital, Tanzania, East Africa - some Australian, some British, a West Indian and a number of East African Jungle Doctors to name but a few.

Scripture quotations taken from the HOLY BIBLE, NEW INTERNATIONAL VERSION. Copyright © 1973, 1978, 1984 by International Bible Society. Used by permission of Hodder & Stoughton Publishers.

Some Scripture quotations are based on the King James Version of the Bible.

African words are used throughout the book, but explained at least once within the text. A glossary is also included at the front of the book along with a key character index.

Contents

Fact File: Paul White

Born in 1910 in Bowral, New South Wales, Australia, Paul had Africa in his blood for as long as he could remember. His father captured his imagination with stories of his experiences in the Boer War which left an indelible impression. His father died of meningitis in army camp in 1915, and he was left an only child without his father at five years of age. He inherited his father's storytelling gift along with a mischievous sense of humour.

He committed his life to Christ as a sixteen-year-old schoolboy and studied medicine as the next step towards missionary work in Africa. Paul and his wife, Mary, left Sydney, with their small son, David, for Tanganyika in 1938. He always thought of this as his life's work but Mary's severe illness forced their early return to Sydney in 1941. Their daughter, Rosemary, was born while they were overseas.

Within weeks of landing in Sydney Paul was invited to begin a weekly radio broadcast which spread throughout Australia as the Jungle Doctor Broadcasts - the last of these was aired in 1985. The weekly scripts for these programmes became the raw material for the Jungle Doctor hospital stories - a series of twenty books.

Paul always said he preferred life to be a 'mixed grill' and so it was: writing, working as a Rheumatologist, public speaking, involvement with many Christian organisations, adapting the fable stories into multiple forms (comic books, audio cassettes, filmstrips), radio and television, and sharing his love of birds with others by producing bird song cassettes - and much more...

The books in part or whole have been translated into 107 languages.

Paul saw that although his plan to work in Africa for life was turned on its head, in God's better planning he was able to reach more people by coming home than by staying. It was a great joy to meet people over the years who told him they were on their way overseas to work in mission because of the books.

Paul's wife, Mary, died after a long illness in 1970. He married Ruth and they had the joy of working together on many new projects. He died in 1992 but the stories and fables continue to attract an enthusiastic readership of all ages.

Fact File: Tanzania

The Jungle Doctor books are based on Paul White's missionary experiences in Tanzania. Today many countries in Africa have gained their independence. This has resulted in a series of name changes. Tanganyika is one such country that has now changed its name to Tanzania.

The name Tanganyika is no longer used formally for the territory. Instead the name Tanganyika is used almost exclusively to mean the lake.

During World War I, what was then Tanganyika came under British military rule. On December 9, 1961 it became independent. In 1964, it joined with the island of Zanzibar to form the United Republic of Tanganyika and Zanzibar, changed later in the year to the United Republic of Tanzania.

It is not only its name that has changed, this area of Africa has gone through many changes since the Jungle Doctor books were first written. Africa itself has changed. Many of the same diseases raise their heads, but treatments have advanced. However new diseases come to take their place and the work goes on.

Missions throughout Africa are often now run by African Christians and not solely by foreign nationals. There are still the same problems to overcome however. The message of the gospel thankfully never changes and brings hope to those who listen and obey. *The Jungle Doctor* books are about this work to bring health and wellbeing to Africa as well as the good news of Jesus Christ and salvation.

Fact File: Typhoid Fever

Typhoid is an illness caused by a particular bacteria that is transmitted by the ingestion of food or water contaminated with faeces from an infected person. The bacteria of the infected person are absorbed into the digestive tract and eliminated with the waste. Typhoid fever is characterized by a sustained fever as high as 40°C (104°F), profuse sweating, gastroenteritis, and diarrhea. Less commonly a rash may appear.

As the disease progresses the patient often suffers from delirium and a rattling sound is heard in the lungs. Diarrhea can occur at this stage. However, constipation is also frequent. The spleen and liver are enlarged and tender. Later on the patient may suffer from intestinal bleeding; intestinal perforation; inflammation of the brain and other organs as well as abscesses. By the end of the third week the fever abates and this continues into the fourth week.

Typhoid fever in most cases is not fatal. Antibiotics have been commonly used to treat it in developed countries. Prompt treatment reduces the case-fatality rate to approximately 1%. When untreated, typhoid fever persists for three weeks to a month. Death occurs in between 10% and 30% of untreated cases.

Sanitation and hygiene are the critical measures that can be taken to prevent typhoid. Typhoid can only spread in environments where human faeces or urine are able to come into contact with food or drinking water. Careful food preparation and washing of hands are therefore crucial to preventing typhoid.

Fact File: Words

WORDS TO ADD EXPRESSION AND EMPHASIS: Eheh, Heh, Hongo, Kah, Koh, Ngheeh, Tichi Yah, Yoh.

TANZANIAN LANGUAGES: Swahili (main language), Chigogo or Gogo (one of the 150 tribal languages)

Askari – Police

Assante – Thank you

Assante sana – Thank you very much

Ati za hako? – What is your news?

Bibi – Grandmother

Boma – Cattle enclosure

Bwana – Male name of respect

Bwete – Worthless

Cidindilo – Jail

Cifuko – Calico bag

Cigongo – Burden

Debe – Four gallon container

Dudus – Insects

Fundi – Expert

Gwe go Mulungo u mulungu lungu – Oh almighty God, Almighty God

Habari gani – What is the news?

Habari njema – The news is good

Hodi – May I enter?

Home lya nzoka – Snake stick

Hulicize – Listen

Icisi – Evil spirit

Ilonda – Ulcer

Ituwi – Owl

Izuguni – The mosquito

10

Kabisa – Absolutely
Karibu – Come in
Katali – Long ago
Kumbe – Behold
Kwaheri – Goodbye
Kweli – Truly
Mafuta – Oil
Mafuta ga simba – Lion's fat
Malenga – Water
Mbeka – Truly
Mbera, Mbera – Quickly
Mbisi – Hyena
Mbukwa – Good morning
Mbungo – Tsetse flies
Mihanya – Good evening
Mikutupa – Tick
Misaa – (Reply to good evening)
Miti – Medicine
Mugoli – The rich one
Mulungo – God, Supreme Being
Mutemi – Chief
Mushenzishenzi – As heathen as can be
Muzungu – European
Ng'o – Never
Ngubi – Warthog
Nhembo – Elephant
Nzoka zono zikufunya – The snake that spits; Cobra
Nyamale – Be quiet
Nzeg-nzeg – Hammock
Nzogolo – The rooster or the second cock crow
Nzoka mbaha – Python
Pole – Gently

Shaitan/Shaitani – The devil

Shauri – Discussion

Sikuku – Celebration

Sunga ku myaka ne cibitila – Until the years that go on and on without end

Topee – Pith helmet

Ulece kogopa mwendece – Don't be frightened, little one

Ulya – Europe

Uze mbera, mwana yunji – Come quickly, another baby

Viswanu – That's good

Vyo notendo – Yes, I will

Wabibi – Female teachers

Wadodo – Little ones

Wadodo waskooli – Little schoolgirls

Waganga – Witchdoctors

Wenji – Very many

Winjile – Enter

Wugali – Porridge

Wujimbi – Beer

Wazungu – Europeans

Yali bahalya – He is over there

Yayagwe – Oh, my mother

Yesu Kriso – Jesus Christ

Zingombe zinhukulu – Cows

Zo wugono wenynu – How did you sleep?

Fact File: Characters

Bwana - Dr White, main character/narrator
Daudi - Hospital manager
James - Hospital staff
Kefa - Hospital staff
Mafuta - Perisi's father
Makaranga - The Chief
Matata - Simba's first wife who died
Mazengo - The great chief of Ugogo
Moto - The Sub chief of Makali
Muganga/Mganga - The Witch-doctor
Perisi - New nurse student
Sechelela/Sechie - Old African Matron
Simba - The hunter

1
We Smell a Lion

Daudi stopped, and sniffed.

'Bwana, there's been a lion about here. Is your nose awake to that strange musty smell?' He held the hurricane lantern close to the ground, and there, clearly visible in the loose sand, were the paw-marks of a lion.'

'*Kah*,' said my African dispenser, 'Bwana, it is recent too, for do you not see where the dust has been wet by the dew? Behold, are not the lion's paw-marks clearly cut?'

Huskily I whispered, 'Listen, Daudi, what's that?'

He lifted the lantern head-high. For five yards around we could see something of the Central African jungle: thornbush, close up to the path along which we were walking. Weird shadows cast by the light of the lantern did nothing to make us feel more comfortable. Then suddenly from the ghostly arms of a baobab tree which stretched above us leafless, came a dark something to crash into the lantern. We were in darkness. Hastily I struck a match just in time to see a wide span of wings disappearing into the night.

Daudi picked up the lantern. 'Bwana, that was *ituwi, the owl.*'

Fortunately the glass of the lantern was not broken. I proceeded to light the wick again.

'*Koh,*' said Daudi, 'behold, Bwana, here in Tanganyika the owl is said to be a bird of witchcraft. Was I not frightened when that happened? *Yoh*, I'm not scared of witchcraft much, Bwana, but suddenly to be in darkness – *eeh!*'

I smiled. 'Yes, Daudi, I know how it feels – all the little hairs at the back of my head stood straight up when that happened.'

'*Koh,*' said Daudi. 'Well, Bwana, I suppose nothing else will happen to us. I'm only thankful, though, that we've got the lantern.'

The thornbush suddenly gave place to breast-high scrub, and outlined in front of us in the starlight was a hill that seemed to rise for no apparent reason from the plains. Great outcrops of granite, some of them as big as a house, were silhouetted against the skyline. I drew Daudi's attention to one particular group of enormous rocks balanced one upon the other, reaching some fifty feet into the air.

'*Yoh,*' said Daudi. 'Bwana, in our tribe we have a story about those rocks. It is said ...' The path suddenly sloped down and our feet sank into the sand of a dry river-bed.

Abruptly Daudi stopped. '*Koh*,' he said. 'Bwana, there's that smell again.' On the cool breeze that comes before dawn again there was the rank smell of musk. Daudi did not seem disposed to go on. I cleared my throat and broke a very uncomfortable silence.

'Daudi, didn't you once tell me that when you hear lions roaring not far away from you, you need have no fear, for no lion would roar unless he had been fed?'

'*H-e-e-e...*' said the African, 'that's just it, Bwana. Can you hear lions roaring now?'

I could see the whites of his eyes standing out in marked contrast to his dark face. Gripping the knobbed stick that he carried in his right hand he moved forward slowly, and then stopped.

'Bwana,' he said, 'do you see it?'

There, clearly marked in the sand, was the paw-mark of a lion. Carefully we followed the spoor from

the river-bed, up the side of the bank, and along a narrow path flanked by vicious-looking thornbush. Again the path broadened out into a clearing, and by the light of the lantern I could see the trampled stalks of what a little while before had been a first-class millet crop. In front of me Daudi stopped and was examining the ground carefully with the lantern. Together we peered at the dust. The crop had been broken down in what must have been a tremendous struggle, and then my African dispenser bent down, pointing to a dark stain.

'Bwana, that's blood.'

Clearly marked were the lion's paw-marks and the imprint of bare feet. Near the edge of the clearing we found parts of a broken spear. The track leading away towards the village was covered with recent footmarks.

'What does the sand tell you, Daudi?'

The African drew in his breath sharply. 'There must have been a fight, Bwana, it looks to me as though the lion was killed and probably the man as well. See, many feet have during the night returned to the village of Ng'ombe.'

'And what about the lion; wouldn't they leave it here?'

'*Hongo*, Bwana, do not those of our tribe say that lion's fat is a very good medicine indeed?' He wrinkled up his nose and with deep scorn said, '*Eeh*, it is medicine of strength, is lion fat.'

I grasped his shoulder.

'Come on, Daudi, let's hurry. It may be that we can do some good in the village over there. The man may not yet be dead.'

I patted the hip pocket of my shorts where was a hypodermic syringe, and an emergency case of injectable drugs. I only wished I had some surgical instruments with me, but the nearest approach that I had to anything of this sort was a safety-razor blade which I kept in the back of my New Testament, which I always carried round with me in the pocket of my shirt.

Daudi was saying something as he walked along briskly ahead of me.

'I'm sorry,' I said. 'I didn't hear what you said. Would you mind saying it again?'

'Bwana, I was telling you how *Muganga*, the witchdoctor, uses lion fat as a medicine amongst the people of our tribe. Suppose, Bwana, you have a pain in your chest, and the witch-doctor is called, then he will take a pair of sandals, spit on them, and throw them on the ground. He then will examine them and tell you the cause of your trouble, and then perhaps after you have paid a bowl of grain for his work with the sandals, he will say, "Will I not be given a cow if I make powerful medicine?"'

'What then, Daudi, if they pay over the cow?'

'*Hongo*, Bwana! Muganga gathers herbs and mixes them with lion fat. That is the *miti,* the medicine, that is rubbed in. *Yoh*, Bwana, see how it is supposed to work. The strength of the lion comes into you, and out goes your pain, and *Kumbe*, if the pain doesn't go from your chest, Muganga says the spell against you must have been a very strong one.'

'*Kumbe*, Daudi.' I raised my eyebrows. 'A cow for that!'

The African dispenser nodded. 'Perhaps also, Bwana, the pain is in your stomach, and you have taken many medicines. Then in the end they will say 'Ah, well, this is a bad thing, it will take a very strong medicine!' and again the sore spot is rubbed with lion's fat, but, *Hongo!* The pain remains, unless, of course, Bwana, it exists in a man's head and not in his stomach.'

'*Koh*,' I said, 'and again you pay a cow, eh?'

'Truly, Bwana,' said Daudi, 'that is the way of our tribe. Behold, until the hospitals came here there was no other medicine. They knew of no other way.'

We walked on in silence for a moment, and then Daudi said: 'Do you remember the meningitis epidemic, Bwana?'

'Do I?' I replied. 'Was I ever so tired in my life?'

'The only medicine which the Muganga has to treat meningitis with is lion fat, Bwana. Our people call this disease "the disease of death", and truly, such it is, for although the medicine is rubbed into your forehead and down your spine,' Daudi shrugged his shoulders, 'you die all the same.'

'But it's a different story now, Daudi, since we started using the sulpha drugs?'

It was gradually getting lighter, and I could see Daudi vigorously nodding his head.

'*Kweli*, Bwana, truly. We have gained much confidence by our hospitals and operations and medicines that work, and by our Christian teaching and preaching. *Yoh*, Bwana, it has made all the difference.'

2
Lion Fat

The path wound through a great grove of baobab trees. Between those huge trunks we could see the village in front of us. As we got closer the long squat houses came into view. But there was none of the usual early morning activity of the men and the small boys driving out the cattle and the goats to pasture. Everybody seemed concentrated in one corner of the village.

Under an umbrella-shaped thorn tree we came upon an animated scene. A group of men with red mud in their hair had just finished skinning the lion, and were about to peg out its skin, while an older, rather gaunt man, with huge ear lobes filled with ornaments reaching halfway down to his shoulders was kneeling beside the carcass and producing handfuls of foul-looking material from the region of the lion's midriff. This he threw into a clay pot and wiped each finger separately in a way that made me feel squeamish. Daudi whispered to me.

'*Mafuta ga simba,* lion's fat, Bwana.'

Someone looked up and for a moment there was a strange, hostile pause.

Finally in Chigogo, the language of the Central Plains of Tanganyika, I said, '*Mbukwa*, good morning.' Some of them jumped to their feet, and replied '*Mbukwa*.'

'*Zo wugono wenynu*, how did you sleep?' I asked.

There came a mumbled and none too friendly answer to this traditional morning greeting.

The witch-doctor stood up, the lion's fat dripping from his claw-like hands. He was not a pretty sight.

'*Mbukwa*,' said I. 'Tell me, who was it that slew the lion?'

'*Yali bahalya*, he is over there', replied the witchdoctor sharply, pointing with his chin towards a mud house on the other side of the village. Abruptly he turned away from me and stepped back to his horrible task.

We walked across towards the narrow wickerwork doorway that had been indicated to us. We were still thirty or forty yards away when a woman suddenly came rushing out with terror written in her eyes, screaming out the piercing alarm signal of the tribe. She stumbled past us unheeding. We broke into a run, pausing for a second to cry: '*Hodi?* May we come in?' before entering the doorway.

A gruff voice from within said '*Winjile!* Enter!' Daudi swiftly went in and more slowly I followed. In the dim light of the mud hut I could see a tall figure lying inert on a cowskin on the floor. Crowded round, squatting on the ground, was a group of old men and women. They were rocking to and fro on their heels and groaning.

Then Daudi, bending down, whispered: 'Bwana, we are too late – he is dead.'

I went on one knee beside the unfortunate hunter, and felt his pulse. There was no beat at his wrist. Then I put my hand on his blood-stained bare chest, and I could feel a faint flicker.

'No, Daudi, he's still alive; perhaps we can save him. Quickly, get boiling water and some blankets.'

Daudi turned quickly to the dazed relatives.

'Behold,' said he, 'the European here is a great doctor. He has the medicines which bring life. He says that, behold, your relation here is not dead, and if there is hot water and if there are blankets he perhaps will be able to bring him along the road to health.'

Several got to their feet and proceeded to do what he asked at a speed which I felt was altogether inadequate. I turned up the wick of the lantern and made a rapid survey of the damage. He had been terribly mauled. I pulled out my handkerchief, and with it managed to control some of the bleeding.

Daudi came running in with a gourd of lukewarm water that was distinctly muddy. Into my syringe I dropped two pellets of morphia and sucked up some of the water into the syringe.

'Daudi,' I said, 'don't you ever do this unless it is an absolute emergency. That water is probably swarming with germs, but unless we get this medicine into him he'll die, and a few germs inside a living man are better than no painkilling medicine inside a dead one.'

Half-a-dozen filthy cotton blankets were brought at that moment, and I covered as much of the patient as I could without bringing those blankets into actual contact with his wounds. There was nothing more that could be done for the moment. I could see some old women blowing into flames a red coal that glowed underneath the great clay pot.

'*Mbera, mbera!*' I called. 'Quickly!'

'*Yoh*,' said one of the old women, looking up, 'there is no profit in hurry. Water will not be heated in that way.'

With the inadequate light of the lantern I made a full survey of his injuries. His left thigh had been badly mauled by the lion, as also had his leg. I could feel a pulse at the hunter's wrist now. An impromptu bed was made up and two small boys armed with branches were given the job of keeping the flies at bay. With the other tube from my stethoscope I poured hot fluids into his system.

'Daudi,' I said, 'what have we got in the way of dressings for this? We've got to have something we can use as a bandage. See if you can find anything round the village.'

He went off at the double and came back a few minutes later.

'Bwana,' he said, 'there is nothing at all – nothing.'

I thought for a moment. ''Well, Daudi, there is only one thing, and that is our shirts.'

'*Koh*,' said Daudi looking at his, which was brand-new khaki drill. 'Bwana, your shirt is of white material and is old. Mine is of khaki material and it is new.'

And so my shirt went into the pot. Actually, Daudi had got two smaller pots from somewhere, so I took off my shirt and tore it into strips. Those strips which could be used as bandages were used as such, and the other bits for swabs, and various other things that would be required. As soon as the shirt and the water was boiling some of it was poured on to the shirt and this in turn was picked up. My razor blade was also boiled. I scrubbed my hands as well as I could without soap, in one of the clay pots which was not made for a handbasin, and then set to work to do a surgical operation which consisted chiefly in cleaning up the wound and getting rid of odds and ends which might contain germs. To perform this procedure accurately and effectively with bare hands and a razor blade is not my idea of surgery. It was not an over easy operation to do under normal conditions, but working by the dim light of the hurricane lantern, with the patient lying on a cowskin on the floor, things could hardly have been more difficult. I could not but notice a cockroach appear from beneath one of the clay pots and scuttle across the floor. Noticeable also were smaller insects, not mentioned in polite company, which I felt were taking an altogether undue interest in me.

Daudi kept up a continual supply of bits of wrung-out shirt. I packed the wound with these, and roughly bandaged the whole. Then I released the tourniquet. The patient gave a long shuddering sigh. I watched my bandages, but there was no obvious sign of haemorrhage.

Then there seemed to be quite a deal of amusement in those who were looking on. I turned round to Daudi and said in English, 'What's the joke, Daudi?'

'Bwana,' he said, 'they are very much interested, for never have they seen so much white skin all at once.' I became acutely aware of my shirtlessness.

The patient was trying to murmur something. '*Malenga!*' he gasped. 'Water!'

I held hot tea to his lips. He gulped some down.

Behind me I heard the high-pitched voice of an old African woman saying, '*Koh*, it's only painted on.'

I could almost feel Daudi's smile as he bent down.

'Bwana,' he said, 'there are those here who think you are like the small boys undergoing the tribal initiation and that the whiteness of your skin is due to pipe-clay.'

I knew it was vital if we were to get our patient carried home that I should gain the goodwill of these people, and I felt that my white skin was as good a method as any other. After I tied the last knot I got to my feet, turned to the old woman, and said:

'*Bibi*, grandmother, have you doubts about my skin?'

'*Yoh*,' said the old woman backing away, 'I have not.'

'Come,' I said smiling, 'do not have doubts, do not be frightened. See, it is all true meat.'

The old woman chuckled and reached out a bony and not too clean finger, scratched tentatively at my shoulderblades, and then came a bit closer to them.

'*Yoh*,' she said. Then having satisfied herself that it was skin and skin only, she turned round to her cronies and said, '*Heh*, aren't Europeans strange-looking creatures?'

'Come,' I said, 'let us not have words. At the moment we need *nzeg-nzeg*, a hammock. If the life of your relative is to be saved he must be carried to our hospital, way over there beyond the thornbush.' I pointed east, African fashion, with my chin.

But for quite a time nobody did anything. 'Daudi,' I said, 'every minute is important. Call the Chief and we will get him to assist.'

But even when he arrived there was considerable trouble in getting the relatives to agree to pay for a cow for his transport to hospital. I saw the injured man's lips move and bent down and heard him whisper, 'Is not a man's life worth that of a cow? Are there not also many cows in my herd and in the herds of my family?'

I stood to my feet and in a loud voice repeated these words. On hearing them his relations, with bad grace, went out to find the creature. In the long delay, which irritated me beyond measure, I coaxed my patient to drink more hot, sweet tea. My finger on his pulse gave me the impression that his condition was improving. At long last the cow was brought, and with it a long bamboo pole. The four carriers took up their positions. The pole was first put above the patient and the blanket upon which he lay folded over and pinned into position with three-inch iron-hard

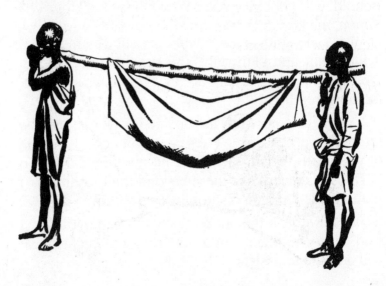

thorns. He was then lifted from the ground and slowly our safari moved on its way back to the hospital. I bade the African villagers a ceremonial farewell, and looking back I saw the lionskin pegged out in the sun, the witch-doctor still busily engaged in preparing lion fat from the carcass.

By now the sun was getting very hot. After an hour's walk we paused under the shade of a great baobab tree. Carefully the patient was put down. I gave another injection. His pulse was rapid and his breathing was most difficult. After ten minutes' rest he rallied a little.

'Bwana,' he said, 'I killed that lion with my spear. It jumped at me but I drove the spear into its heart. *Kah*, Bwana, but its claws tore me. Behold, the pain is very great. Let me die.'

'There is no need for you to die. *Heh*, rather let me repair you so that you may live to kill more lions. Behold, will I not give you a new name? I will call you *Simba*, the lion, after the king of the jungle whom you slew in fair fight today.'

The carriers chuckled and nodded their heads. '*Heh, heh*, Bwana, those are good words.'

Two hot, weary hours later Simba lay between the white sheets of a bed in our hospital. Only one possible treatment stood between him and death, and that was blood transfusion. I went to the bearers who carried him in.

'Listen,' I said, 'we can save Simba if you will give some of your blood. It merely means pushing a needle into your veins. There is no danger. There is a little pain, and in this simple way you may save the life of this brave man.'

For a moment they stared at each other open-mouthed, then one of them spoke hastily, 'No, Bwana, we refuse, it is not our custom.'

Neither pleas, scorn nor argument had any effect on this group of African men. Quite a crowd had gathered to hear what was going on, amongst them some of the girls who had trained as teachers at our C.M.S. schools just beyond the hill. They had been visiting at the hospital. One of them, Perisi by name, said, 'Bwana, if you took some blood from me would I be able to teach in school tomorrow?'

'*Hongo!* Yes. You may feel a little dizzy for half an hour or so but nothing more.'

'Then take my blood, Bwana,' she said.

'But,' broke in one of the men who had carried Simba in, 'you are no relation of his.'

'*Kah*,' said Perisi. 'Would I see a man die when I can help him?'

Hurriedly I made the necessary tests and within half an hour I had collected a large pickle-bottle full of blood which could well mean the life of Simba.

'Lie there, Perisi,' I said, 'while I give it to this hunter of ours. You'll feel all right soon.'

'*Kah*, Bwana,' she said, 'it is my blood, can I not see you give it to him? Bwana, this is a small thing to ask.'

And so, sitting on a chair, she watched her own blood being run into the veins of the muscular hunter who was very close to the gates of death. A quarter of the blood had run into his veins when a quiver went through his system. His pulse seemed to me to be improving. With half the bottle empty he yawned.

'Quietly, Simba,' I said. 'Do not move, my friend. Just lie there.'

When the transfusion was nearly completed he opened his eyes – eyes which were not a pretty sight; eye trouble is all too common in those central plains of Tanganyika. He looked across at me.

'Bwana, what are you doing? What is that?'

'It's blood,' I said, 'blood that has been given to you to save your life.'

'But, Bwana, who gave it?'

With my hands engaged with juggling with needles and rubber tubes I pointed with my chin towards the African girl sitting in the chair beneath the window. 'Perisi, she gave it to you.'

'But why?'

The African girl who had been sitting quietly through the whole proceeding answered quickly, 'Did not the Bwana *Yesu Kristo*, Jesus Christ, give His life for me that I might live? Shall I not give my blood that you may live?'

Simba looked dazed and closed his swollen eyelids. 'I cannot understand,' he said.

'Don't try,' I suggested, 'but later on you will.'

I disconnected the apparatus. For the hundredth time that day my fingers felt the artery at his wrist. It was beating forcefully and with the regularity of a clock. I turned to thank Perisi for what she had done, but she had quietly slipped away.

3

Lion Hunter is Repaired

Three weeks passed. Propped up, smiling, in the third bed was my old friend "lion's meat."

'*Mbukwa*, Simba.'

'*Mbukwa*, Bwana,' grinned the cheerful hunter.

'What's the news?' I asked.

James had removed the bandages, and was taking off the dressing from our patient's legs. The whole wound had healed up beautifully. With a few skin grafts he would be able to be up and about within a month. All the time we had been treating his eyes, which were in a dreadful state. Day by day drops had gone into them and there was a definite improvement at last. I put my hand on his shoulder.

'Listen, Simba. Your legs are a small problem compared with your eyes. But if you have patience, and can stand some more pain I will have your eyes back to normal before long, if you will help.'

Now Simba was a cheerful person. His laugh re-echoed through the wards. He grasped my hand in both of his.

'Bwana,' said he, 'was there no pain in this leg? Do I not know that, because of you, I am alive? Will I not do everything you say, pain or no pain?'

'Bwana,' said Kefa, 'there is much work in this ward, and it takes up half-an-hour, three times a day, to wash out his eyes, as you have instructed. Behold, I have a new method. Will you agree?'

He took me outside, and showed me a wide-necked bottle fitted up with sundry glass tubes. He up-ended this, and a fine trickle of lotion ran out.

'Behold, Bwana, Simba can do this himself. It will please him and save us time.'

'But Kefa,' I said, 'who will catch the water? Will it not make a mess?'

'Bwana, he can go and sit in the peanut plantation, and behold any water that is spilled will be helpful to the garden.'

And so it came about, that Simba was to be seen each day, sitting amongst the peanuts, washing his eyes with this lotion. I painted the lids, and anointed the angry-looking areas with ointment with real results. At last the day came for the final skingraft, and I wrote in the report, 'His eyes have a normal appearance.'

His eyelashes, however, turned in, and irritated the eyeball exceedingly. Every fourth day I plucked them. I don't know whether it was a very painful proceeding. However, as each hair came out, he would emit a terrific roar, and send the rest of his ward-fellows into fits of laughter. Then he would pitch the story of how he would rather face a score of lions than one doctor, armed with a little pair of forceps.

'You see, Bwana,' said he, 'I can stick spears into lions, but it is not the custom to do that to doctors, and so, behold, you cause me to suffer, and I can do nothing but roar.'

Kefa was just about to put drops into his eyes when my patient, for good measure, opened his mouth and produced a final bellow.

I took the opportunity of putting eyedrops into the wrong spot! The ward rocked with mirth, while Simba coughed and spluttered, and then the whole bed shook with his laughter. He was one of the most cheerful souls in the whole place.

At first he had come to church in a bed, carried down by the dressers, and placed at the back. Then he limped down with Kefa's arm supporting him.

One day I came to the ward, and found him laboriously spelling out, word by word, a passage from the New Testament.

'Behold, Bwana,' said he, 'here's poor old "lion" becoming a scholar! Before long with my repaired eyes, I will be able to read, and to know of God as never before.'

That day I did his first operation, which involved a little surgical fancywork to the skin of his eyelid. It was an operation I had never done before, and I had the chance of using a story that I had heard in my hospital days.

Simba walked to the theatre. His legs were normal now, but large scars indicated the damage done by the lion's claws. Going into the theatre he sniffed!

'*Kah!* What a smell these places have!'

Seeing me, he grasped Daudi's arm and with a broad smile on his face and his knees knocking together in the most amazing fashion he said:

'*Kumbe!* I am frightened. *Yah!* He will hurt me! *Kah!* I have never had an operation on my eyes before. I am frightened.'

I beckoned to Daudi. 'Tell him that if he is frightened it is nothing to what I feel. Behold, it is the first time I have ever done this operation!'

The dispenser burst into laughter, and the theatre rocked, when the message was passed on to the victim.

When all was quiet I said, 'Listen! We rejoice in much fun. But these eyes belong to our friend here and upon me is the responsibility of fixing them. Should I make a mistake, damage will be done; damage which will affect him all his life. That is why I am now going to ask God, who is my Father and who helps me in all things, to guide my hand as I repair these eyelids.'

As I ended my brief prayer, the deep voice of my patient broke in: 'Thank you, God, for the Bwana. Thank you for the medicines, and just help me to understand all your words.'

There was not a flicker from Simba right through the operation and I will admit its extreme difficulty, in the hands of a novice at that particular job. But as I put in the last stitch and tied the last knot, I felt that although perhaps it was not the neatest of jobs at least it would produce results.

Next morning, in the wards, I found Simba, eyes bandaged, but cheerful, singing at the top of his voice.

'*Nyamale*, be quiet,' said Kefa. 'You'll tear your stitches.'

'*Kumbe*,' came the retort, 'whose stitches are they?'

'Mine,' I replied from the doorway, 'for I put them in.'

'*Yeh!*' said Simba. 'Behold, I didn't know you were there, Bwana!'

'Perhaps not,' said Kefa, 'but the Bwana's got his largest needle this time, and it's threaded with string and he won't sew up your eye only. It'll be your mouth!'

Chuckles came from all round the ward.

I scrubbed my hands and watched the junior dresser carefully putting the water round some cherished tomatoes which grew in the courtyard. Kefa followed my glance and smiled.

'Never a thing goes to waste here, Bwana. All the used water goes on to the vegetables; all the blankets go sides to middle when they wear; the old sheets become first, pillowslips, and then end their lives as bandages. Truly, Bwana, we are cautious.'

'We've got to be, Kefa. We're terribly short of stuff, and haven't enough money to pay next month's wages. You see, we're so far from my home country that the people there don't realise that we have needs, and are almost at our last shilling. Now, if they could see Simba here...'

'Bwana,' said Daudi, 'we've repaired the work of a lion for seven shillings; we've fixed the trouble brought by mosquitoes for three more, and now we'll give him back his sight and give him proper eyelids again for ten shillings.'

Simba overheard this last remark, and laughed.

'Me, worth a pair of shoes? *Kah!* Bwana, take the shoes.'

The staff grinned broadly, but I was gripped with the seriousness of things.

'Simba, my friend, if you were just so much flesh and bone I might agree, but what about your soul? Your body can be killed by a selection of things ranging from lions to mosquitoes, but your *mutima*, your soul, lives on.'

'Kefa was unbandaging his head, and I waited, forceps poised for action. Off came the pad and the gauze.

'*Yah*,' said Daudi. 'Have all the stitches been pulled out? Is it a dreadful mess?'

For answer I swabbed the area with lotion, and pointed with the forceps to a row of stitches, all in place – no infection visible. Everything was as it ought to have been.

Above the wound a large, rather bloodshot red eye opened and blinked at me. I nodded in reply to its unasked question.

'Yes, Simba. All's well. Nothing will remain except a half-inch scar.'

'*Assante Sana*, thank you very much,' he replied. '*Yah!* I have much to be thankful for. Behold, Bwana, I will pay for this work with one of my cows.'

Kefa, who was listening quietly, suddenly broke in:

'You can pay money for cows, for repairs to be done to your legs or eyes when there is need, but no money or animal can pay for the surgery to your soul.'

The whole of my star patient's face was wrinkled in amazement.

'Without money and price, Simba, is the price you pay for getting rid of sin from your soul. Jesus Christ paid the highest possible price – His own life!'

'And,' broke in Kefa, 'He asks you to believe in Him. That means to be absolutely loyal to Him, and then to follow and obey His instructions without question.'

Kefa had a Bible in his hand.

'Bwana,' said Simba, 'with my repaired eyes I can soon read God's book for myself and think of these things and understand them.'

'Yes,' I said, 'and, I hope, act upon them.'

Then came the day when Simba was ready to go home. We said goodbye to him at the gate and he waved his hand as he walked along the path that Daudi and I had so eventfully travelled some weeks before.

'*Koh*, Bwana,' said Daudi, 'I wonder if we'll ever hear of him again.'

4

The Lion and the Snakes

'*Kumbe*, Bwana,' said Daudi. 'A man has arrived here at Mvumi today who has a story to tell. *Heeh!* His coming brings much interest into life.'

I was just blowing the bubbles out of a syringe and preparing to inject an African man who lay in bed. 'Who is it, Daudi?' The dispenser rubbed the skin with a swab soaked in methylated spirit, and grinned.

'*Heeh*, Bwana, it is our old friend, Simba.'

'*Hongo!* The man we had in this bed about a year ago who was mauled by a lion, who was saved by a blood transfusion – that chap?'

'*Yah*,' said the patient seeing the needle getting closer to him. '*Yah*, am I not going to be bitten? But, Bwana, eek...'

'Ah,' said Daudi, 'it didn't hurt.'

'*Kumbe*,' said the patient, 'into whose arm did it go, yours or mine?'

'*Yah*,' laughed the African dispenser, 'I didn't feel a thing.' He rubbed the spot where the needle had been a second or so before.

'*Yah*,' he said, 'you would have had something to complain of if you'd been like Simba. Behold, his leg was torn from the knee right up.'

At that moment a smiling face appeared through the door.

'*Mbukwa*, Simba,' I said. 'Good day!' The African came in and shook me very firmly by the hand.

'*Yah*, Bwana, it is good to see you and to be back here.'

He looked across at the man in the bed. 'Bwana, *heeh*, do I not remember the days that I lay there.' He looked at the rough-cut rafters. 'Bwana, how often have I looked at those? Did they not seem to twist and twirl as the pain came over me? Behold, I would look up at Daudi here and he would suddenly seem to disappear in a cloud. But, *heeh*, all was different when you gave me the blood from the bottle.'

'*Kumbe*,' said Daudi, 'that was the day. Behold, that day we thought you were dead.'

'You would have been dead, too,' I said, 'if it hadn't been for Perisi, who gave you that blood.'

'*Hongo*,' said Simba, 'do I not remember? Look, Bwana.' He drew from behind his back a parcel all wrapped up and tied Indian-fashion with yards and yards of cotton. From it he produced two lengths of colourful cotton material, such as the African women wear. 'Behold, I am going to present these to Perisi. I said thank you with my mouth, when I left, but,

42

behold, now I am saying thank you with my gifts. Behold, these days I have much money.'

'*Ehh!*' said Daudi. 'What is your work?'

'*Kah*, what a job I've got. And what a Bwana I've been serving. *Ahhhhhhh!*'

Simba shook his head and rolled his eyes in the most amusing fashion, and then as mysteriously as he had produced the parcel he pulled out a bag – a rather soiled-looking bag made from tough canvas. He pulled the string and poured on to the floor a stream of African shillings.

'*Kah*,' I said, seeing them spill out over the floor. 'You are *Mugoli* – the rich one.'

Simba laughed a very hearty laugh. '*Heeh*, Bwana, these shillings are not mine at all.'

'What!' I said. 'Whose are they?'

'Bwana,' said the African – he stood up and spoke more quietly. 'These are God's shillings.'

'Oh?' I said, questioningly.

Simba went on. 'Bwana, when I lay in that bed, behold one day you came in and read from God's Word. They were the words of the prophet who wrote the last words of the Old Testament.'

'*Kah*,' said Daudi, 'I remember that, Bwana. Was it not the day when the boys stole the mangoes from your tree, and behold they ate too many and they came to the hospital, and were violently sick? We all thought it was very funny.'

'Yes,' said Simba, interrupting, 'and we started talking about stealing and then, Bwana, we talked of people who robbed God. I asked how this could be and you read these words, "Will a man rob God? Yet you rob me. But you ask, 'How do we rob you?' In tithes and offerings." *Hah*, Bwana, and when you got as far as that did we not say "What are tithes and offerings?" and you told how in the days when the words were written it was the custom of the people to give God one gourd full of their crop out of every ten that they had and one calf of every ten born in their herd; you explained to us that when thanks stayed at mere words they robbed God.'

The whole incident was very clear in my mind. I nodded and Simba went on: 'Then Bwana, you read "Bring the whole tithe into the storehouse. Test me in this, says the Lord Almighty, and see if I will not throw open the floodgates of heaven and pour out so much blessing that you will not have room enough for it."

'*Kah*, Bwana, those words were written for me on a piece of paper and I said them over and over, until they stayed there.' He patted himself on the back of the head. 'Behold, I have kept here one shilling out of every ten that I earned in my work and in the collecting of them, and in the giving of them to God I have great joy. Behold, was not my life saved here? Shall I not give to help save others from pain and perhaps death?'

Daudi had counted the money into neat piles. There were fifty-two shillings. 'Behold,' he said, 'Bwana, there is enough money here for us to save five people's lives and a bit over.'

'*Yah*,' said Simba. 'Bwana, that is joy. Is not that more fun than buying many things that you eat and wear. *Kah*, and what fun it's been earning it. Let me tell you the story…'

At that moment an African nurse rushed through the door.

'Bwana,' she gasped, '*uze mbera – mwana yunji*, another baby.'

As I went through the door, I said, 'Simba, I will use the two shillings of your fifty-two so that this child may be safely born and the mother looked after, and if it's a boy I'll get her to call it Simba, after you.'

An hour later I went round to the dispensary. 'Behold,' I said, 'that child has been born into the world and his name is Simbambili – lion the second.'

Simba was watching Daudi count out hundreds of pills. 'Bwana,' he said, 'behold, *heeh*, I have joy.' He was leaning on a six-foot stick that was forked at one end. He held it out towards me. 'Behold this is my *home lya nzoka*.'

'What?' I wrinkled my forehead in my effort to translate. 'Your snake stick?'

Simba nodded vigorously. '*Yeh*, Bwana, these days have I not been working for a *Muzungu*, a European, who hunts snakes? Am I not his *fundi* – his expert? Can I not catch snakes? *Yah*, Bwana, snakes whether they be big or small. *Heeh*, you should see me catch them and put them in a bag or in a box. *Heeh*, it is a sight to make your eyes glad.'

'*Hongo*,' I said, 'I don't like snakes, large or small.'

'*Kah*, Bwana,' said Simba, 'snakes are not really bad if you can tame them. *Heeh*, they become pets so easily. You can keep them in the house to eat the rats. They are very good indeed at catching rats.'

'*Yah*,' said Daudi, 'I'd rather have rats!'

'Now,' said Simba, 'my Bwana did not want dead snakes, he wanted live ones.'

'Come on,' I said, settling down to mix up some cough mixture, 'tell us about the biggest snake you caught.'

'*Hongo*,' said Simba smiling, 'Bwana, the biggest snake we caught was *nzoka mbaha*.' (Daudi interpreted in a hoarse whisper, 'Python, Bwana'). Simba nodded. 'Bwana, If you would care to catch one of these snakes, behold, you need four men and you go out early in the morning when it is cold. Behold, the snakes are sleepy and they do not move fast.'

'*Yoh!*' cried Daudi, looking up from his weighing machine. 'In words it is easy, but what of the hunt?'

Simba held up a finger. 'Listen, O medicine mixer. We went out into the jungle and came to a place of many rocks. The orders were that we should go quietly for it was the place of many snakes. Then we saw a huge python. The Bwana called us aside and whispered in our ears. To me, he said, 'Grasp the snake by the head and lift.' He himself was to take the tail; the others (they had not much strength) were to grasp the body

of the snake and lift it off the ground and straighten it out. *Heeh*, and then he said we were to carry it to an open place. We would put it in a very large sack. Behold, Bwana, we crept towards that snake very quietly. Suddenly the Bwana raised his hand. I leapt and grasped that snake very close to its head. He got it by the tail. *Yah*, and did it struggle! *Eeh*, sand flew everywhere. Some of the men were knocked flying. The Bwana had to struggle to hold the tail off the ground, but we got it into the bag. *Yoh!* It was work.' Simba shook his head and rolled his eyes.

'Never let go of a snake's tail too quickly. The Bwana did and *Yah*, did he have trouble! But, Bwana, behold, we got it into the bag in the end. *Heeh*, and that snake has now gone to *Ulya*, Europe.'

At that moment a nurse's head came round the door. 'Bwana,' she panted.

'Yes,' I said, 'I know – another baby. Right, I'm coming.'

'Bwana,' said Simba, 'your work is almost as bad as catching snakes.'

'*Kah*,' I replied, 'if you caught as many snakes as we catch babies in this hospital, why, you'd catch eight hundred in a year!'

Two days later I came into the ward. Into my hand was put a letter written African fashion. It read: 'The Bwana is invited to eat of the goat that is the gift of Simba, the snake-catcher.'

'When will the food be eaten?' I asked.

'Bwana,' said Kefa, putting his hands straight out in front of him, 'it will be at the time when the sun sinks over the edge of the hills.'

I nodded. 'Right, I'll come.'

As the sun set I put on a pair of long trousers, and my mosquito boots, leather affairs that came right up to my knees, and walked up to the hospital. There was an animated scene round a large fire. The crank handle of the car had been fitted to the end of a long green stick. The carcass of the goat was being turned industriously. The light from the fire lit up many expectant faces. The

nurses were there and some of the teachers from the school – among them I noticed Perisi. She was wearing the new cloth which had been given her by the African snake-hunter. I went across to her.

'*Mihanya*, good evening.'

'*Misaa*,' she replied and smiled, a most attractive smile.

'Perisi,' I said, 'It was worth doing what you did for Simba.'

'Bwana,' she said, 'never was a pint of blood better used than on that day. Behold, I did not feel the loss of it much then and not at all now. I hope then that by saving his ordinary life the chance might come to help him to find eternal life.'

Simba was supervising the goat-roasting, his laughter was highly infectious.

'*Heh*,' smiled Perisi, 'is he not fun? His stories of snake-catching – you should hear them!' They were lifting the meat off the fire. The African girl laughed. 'Bwana, truly tonight is a night of joy. Did you see the gift he brought me?'

'Yes,' I said. 'Simba believes not only in saying thank you, but in tying up his thanks in a parcel.'

Daudi and Simba were coming across hurriedly to greet me. The latter was carrying a three-legged stool. He placed it in position before me and a great dish of rice was brought. Daudi had already set to work on the roast goat, slicing it up for the guests.

'Before you eat,' I said, 'here in the light of the fire let us thank God. Simba, have you things to thank God for?'

'Bwana,' he said, 'I do not thank God only for the meat and the food that we are to eat, but I thank Him for my life, which was saved in the hospital here. I thank Him not only for the life that wears out when my body goes, but for the life that goes on and on. *Sunga ku myaka ne cibitila*, until the years that go on and on and on without end.'

Quietly we bowed our heads and thanked God and then we set to. For a while everybody was too busy to talk much but jokes here and there were cracked, and everyone laughed when the plumpest of nurses, in trying to get a chop more than she deserved, burnt her fingers, fortunately not severely, on some hot fat.

'Bwana,' said Daudi, 'behold we would like to hear from Simba how he catches *nzoka zono zikufunya*, the snake that spits.'

'The cobra, eh?' I said in English. Daudi nodded. Speaking in Chigogo I said to Simba: 'Tell us, how do you catch the snake that spits?'

Some light wood was put on to the fire, and in the brightness of the flames Simba stood up and told the story.

'Bwana,' he said, 'once again I have my snake stick.' He produced this stick with its knobbed end. 'You see the snake, and you place the fork over its neck.'

'*Kumbe*,' said I, 'and the snake just waits there for you to do it?'

His eyes rolled in his head, the whites of them contrasting sharply with the blackness of his skin. 'Eh, Bwana, behold it takes much time and there are three of us, and when you have it round his neck, behold, does not the body wriggle very strongly? You thrust the neck hard into the ground, and the Bwana yells, "Do not kill the snake! Do not kill the snake! *Pole! Pole!* Gently!" and then he comes with a noose made of strong string. This he pushes round the neck of *nzoka*, and tightens it very slowly. *Kah*, Bwana, then he grips the snake by the back of the neck and you take off the noose.'

'*Kah*,' I said, 'but does not the reptile struggle?'

'*Heeh*, Bwana, does it not struggle!' Simba's eyebrows reached his hair margin. 'But you hold it round the neck with one hand and the middle of the body with the other and then, Bwana, you have the snake safely.'

Suddenly Simba turned to me. 'Bwana,' he said, 'you tell us a story about snakes.' I had been expecting this, so I said, 'Would you like to hear the story of the Indian snake-charmer, and the snake that he caught when it was very small?' A chorus of affirmatives in three languages came from those crouching around the fire.

'Behold, it was one of the great snakes that do not bite, the snakes that have great strength in their body, and that crush whole goats and swallow them.'

'*Kah*,' said Simba, 'Bwana, we have caught many of those.'

'Well,' I said, 'this snake-charmer caught his snake when it was very small. He trained it and he tamed it and taught it first to coil around his hand. He played strange music to it on his pipe, which was a sort of a flute, and it swayed its head to and fro, keeping time with the music. The snake grew and soon he taught it to coil right round the whole of his arm, and its head swayed to the playing of the strange music. And then as it grew bigger, he taught it to coil around his leg, and once again it was calmed by the music of his flute. Then it became a large snake and he taught it to coil around his body. It would cover the whole of him to his middle. It would wave to and fro as he played the flute. Behold, it was very tame, and when it had grown to its full height, it would coil round the whole of that Indian, and there were others who played the flute, so that the snake would move to and fro with the music.

Many people came to see him do his work. Behold, they paid money to see him and his snake. Many would say to themselves, "*Kumbe!* This is a wonderful thing." And when the man heard them he said, "It is not a wonderful thing. Is not the snake tame? I have had it since it was small. It is my servant." And then the Indian, to make things more dramatic and to gain more money, was accustomed to make noises and to scream when the snake covered him, as though he was being crushed. *Yah*, the people cheered! They said it was a good act. They gave him more money. But still the man smiled within his own heart, and said, Behold, the snake is my servant, he obeys the music of the flute, and when I whistle softly he crawls back again and goes into his own great basket.

'One day the flute was playing. The snake came out of its basket. It coiled gently round the man till he was entirely covered, and then the man screamed, and the people clapped, and said, "*Heeh*, it is a very good act." But the man screamed very strongly and the people who watched had horror, for they saw that, behold, the snake had not answered the music of the flute, nor the whistle of the man. The man who said that the snake was his plaything, his servant, was dead, because of the power of the snake which he thought he had tamed.'

The flames of the fire had burnt down. The Africans sat looking into the glowing embers. 'Behold,' I said, 'the name of the snake was sin. It started as a small thing, it grew, it was the man's plaything, his servant, as he thought. He thought he could control it, but...'

5

The Arrow

The feast was over, the fire that had roasted the goat was now just a glimmer of red amongst the ashes. From where I stood I could see night nurses walking round the hospital with their hurricane lanterns. Beyond the operating theatre the plains of Central Tanganyika showed up white with hills and thornbush like the deep shadows on an etching.

A voice came at my elbow. 'Bwana.'

I didn't turn and look at him because in the moonlight I could see a long shadow of a very muscular man leaning on a hunting spear. The shadow made him look gigantic. I recognised who it was at once.

'Well, Simba, my friend,' I said, 'what is the trouble? Have you eaten too much goat stew or is your leg aching as it does when there is a thunderstorm about, or is it that your eyes which I touched up for you are giving trouble, and you want some black eye drops?'

'Bwana,' said the African very quietly, 'my trouble is not of the body, but it is somewhere here within me.' He put a large hand in the centre of his chest.

'Come,' I said, 'it was those goat chops you ate. Behold, they have upset your stomach. You must need the white medicine.'

'*Kah*, Bwana,' said the African, 'my stomach could eat more than goat. Behold even zebra did not upset that. Bwana, I do not know what to do.' He leaned on his spear and shook his head dejectedly.

'Tell me, Simba, is it that you are not happy in your heart? Once you spoke to me in this very same way over there by the dispensary, and you said you did not see how God could take an interest in you, that He had so many things to think about, so very much to do.'

The African shook his head again. 'Bwana, I understand now, perfectly, and it is because I understand this that I now do not know what to do. You see, Bwana, when you told me about Jesus and you explained how He was the Good Shepherd, and He would give His life for the sheep, you told me how He had given His life for me. Then I decided that I would be His and His only. So, Bwana, now I do not know what to do.'

'Come and sit in my house, where the mosquitoes will not bite us; and tell me all about it.'

He walked behind me along the narrow path that led a quarter of a mile from the hospital to my jungle home. I put the hurricane lantern down on my desk and pulled up a three-legged stool for him to sit on.

'Simba, before you think of the various troubles and worries that are yours, it is always good to ask

God to help and to guide. Very often I pray this prayer, "Oh, Lord, hold up my goings in your paths that my feet don't slip."'

Quietly we bowed our heads. Then Simba said, 'Bwana, in the days before I met you, behold I had a wife whose name was Matata; she cooked my food and helped me dig in the garden, but she was a woman of words. When I went out hunting she would complain. If I stayed home, again she would complain; behold, Bwana, life had no joy in it because of her continual complaining and her many words. *Yoh*, I was wretched! And then she went to see her relations who live over there.' (He pointed with his chin in a direction west.) 'She was gone for two days and then news came that she had the stabbing disease.'

By this I knew that he meant pleurisy.

'Bwana, I made a day and night safari through the jungle. I travelled without stopping, but, Bwana, the disease was too great. I arrived only in time to bid her farewell before she made her last great journey.'

He sat down for a moment. In the distance I could hear the singing of Africans round the camp-fire and the peculiar rhythm of their drums; from near at hand came the howl of a hyena.

Simba continued, 'Bwana, these days I have loneliness in my heart, and I say to myself, should I not marry again? But if I do marry, should I marry a woman of words, like Matata? What should I do, Bwana? My mind goes round and round. *Yah!* My thoughts are full of clouds and mists. I do not know what to do.'

I nodded. 'But Simba, you have ideas?'

'Bwana,' said the African, looking as though he didn't know quite where to put his hands, 'things are different now. I married Matata because I needed a woman to cook for me, to look after my house. Behold, she had strong shoulders, and could carry much wood from the forest for the fire. She could also garden very well. Behold, my relations said, she is a strong woman, and a strong woman who is a good cook and a good gardener will be a good wife. But, Bwana, these days things are different. I – I...' He waved his arms vaguely and put his hand again over the middle of his chest.

'Listen, Simba,' I said, 'when you see the lightning you know there will be...'

'Thunder, Bwana.'

'And when you see the baobab trees come out in leaf you know...'

'Bwana, that the rains are coming.'

'Right,' I said, 'and these days I have used my eyes too! Have I not seen this thing when you first lay in hospital dying, and your life was saved by the blood of Perisi a year ago?'

'Behold, Bwana,' said the African, 'I could not understand why she should do it. Then I saw, Bwana, that she was different; she was not like the women of my village and I understood that it was because she had the love of God in her heart. Bwana, I have walked through the jungle and travelled to and fro. As I have sat by the camp-fire at night, behold, has not my heart called for Perisi? I do not seek a woman just to cook my food, but, Bwana, I seek someone...' He gazed vaguely into the air. 'I cannot find words for it.'

'Simba,' I said, 'God's Book says 'How can two walk together unless they are agreed?'

Simba nodded. 'Does that not mean for those who follow His ways?'

'Truly,' I replied. 'How can people living together be happy if each is trying to travel a different road? Does not God's Book also say: "Do not be yoked together with unbelievers"? Behold, God warns us that there is not profit if you link your life with one who does not follow His ways.'

'Truly, Bwana, they are words of wisdom,' said Simba.

'They are words of wisdom and more – they are orders for those who follow the way of God and Jesus Christ. But those who follow the wishes of their own minds without thinking of the words of God, they find much trouble all their days.'

'*Yah*,' said Simba. 'How I know it, Bwana, but when I approached the father of Matata I had no fears within my heart, but now … my heart trembles within me, my knees feel weak. *Eeeh!*'

'*Kumbe*,' I said, 'is there any profit in standing back waiting for the lion to jump at you? Is it not better to go yourself and talk with her relations? See what dowry they want.'

'Bwana,' said Simba, 'it is not our custom to do these things. Daudi has already done that, and her father says the dowry will be thirty cows. Bwana, I have but ten cows.'

'But you can make more money so that you can buy more cows. So why don't you go and talk to Perisi?

Wouldn't it be best to find out whether she would be willing to be your wife? This may not be the way of the tribe, but it is the way of the heart.'

'Bwana,' said Simba, 'my heart calls for Perisi, but this is a hard thing. Behold, my tongue refuses to move. Did I not see her this evening, but there were no words. It is much easier to hunt a wild animal with a spear or to catch a snake with my forked stick. That, Bwana, is action, but...'

At that moment a startled voice fell on our ears.

'Bwana, come quickly, at the school there is *nzoka*, a snake, in the room of the *wadodo*, the little ones.'

'That, Simba,' I said, jumping to my feet, 'is the place where Perisi looks after the very small children. Here is action. Run!'

I have seldom seen anyone move faster. Simba was there twenty yards ahead of me. He was into the room in a flash. In fifty seconds there was dead cobra in the room where the small African girls had burrowed down beneath blankets and lay shivering with fear.

'*Kah*,' said Simba panting, 'you need have no fear, children; behold, the snake is with its ancestors.'

'*Assante* (thank you), Bwana,' said a quiet-voiced girl standing near the door.

I saw that it was Perisi.

'Don't thank me,' I said. 'It was my friend here, the snake-killer, the lion man, who did it; and behold, Perisi, he would have words with you. I will wait on the veranda for a while as he speaks to you.'

Simba held the dead snake on the end of his stick and he paused uncertainly in the moonlight and then threw the reptile into the peanut gardens.

Then in a soft voice he spoke to the girl.

I walked up and down on the veranda. After a while I saw Perisi turn away, walk into the room, and close the door. Simba, taking up his spear, ran across the courtyard, vaulted over the stone fence and ran towards the village.

I ran out. '*Heeh!*' I said. 'Hey, Simba, what happened? What did she say?' But tantalisingly he disappeared into the darkness.

6

Targets

Daudi was assisting me to carry large bottles of medicine. We were both badly overloaded.

He put a huge bottle on the ground, and said: 'Bwana, here comes our friend, Simba. It looks as though he has something to say.'

'*Hoh!*' I replied. '*Heeh*, old Simba has the courage of a lion, but there is fear in his heart since…'

'Bwana, in our country it is not usual for a man to love his wife. She is cook, gardener, and childminder. But it is different here. Simba is in love. And badly!'

'Three days ago, Daudi, he came with me to the girls' school and killed a snake. I knew he would have words with Perisi, so I arranged things. They talked for a few minutes, then she went into a room and shut the door, and he ran away as though all the jungle were after him. I called out, "Stop! Stop!" and I thought then there must have been trouble somewhere.'

Daudi laughed. 'Bwana, Sechelela is an old woman of great wisdom. She understands these things. She called Perisi up to see her and talked very quietly and behold, the girl too, has the trouble. She sighs and has no appetite. She says that for many days her heart has been calling, calling for Simba.'

'Quietly, Daudi! He's within hearing distance now; let's hear what's doing.'

I turned to the hunter.

'Well,' I said, 'you're a nice one, to run away the other day without telling me what had happened.'

'*Kah*,' said Simba, 'some people say what they think about a thing, others talk in proverbs. I wanted to think, Bwana, so I ran into the jungle and sat.'

'*Heeh*,' I said, 'therefore she must have said something to you which was not "No."'

'Bwana,' said the African, 'that's just it. She listened to my words, and Bwana, they came on slow and heavy feet, and when I had said them she turned to me and said, "When I planted my seed in the garden, behold, I had no corn cob to roast, for then the shoots were still small and green." She said that, Bwana, and then she walked inside the door and shut it, and I ran away to sit in the jungle and think and think.'

'*Kah*,' said Daudi, 'surely you know what that means.'

'It could mean many things,' sighed Simba, 'many things.'

'*Heeh*,' said Daudi. 'Bwana, it is an African way of saying that she would make sure that Simba had real faith in God. Behold, his days of belief are few, he has done little for God. How is she to be sure, that if she married him she would not be marrying trouble?'

'*Kah*,' said Simba, '*heeh*, then what must I do?'

'Beyond the place where you killed the lion is a village, a place where the witch-doctor rules. No one comes here from that place: children are blinded, babies die, people suffer.'

'*Kah*, Bwana, that is true. Do we not call it *Makali*, the place of fierceness?' said Daudi.

'Listen, Simba, that is the place where I plan to put a new branch hospital and school. It…'

'*Hongo*, Bwana, but who would go there? It is a place of great danger. Spells would be cast. *Ehh!* It is a place where Shaitan, the devil, has great freedom.'

'You, Simba, could go there.'

'I, Bwana, but…'

'You had no fear of the lion and the python, do you fear the people of your own tribe?'

Simba shook his head doubtfully. 'Bwana, I am a hunter, not a teacher. How could I do this thing?'

'When you plant peanuts, Simba, first you cultivate the ground, then you put in the seed. It grows silently under the soil. Its leaves are the colour of grass. It is not greatly noticed, and then the fruits appear in its roots … understand?'

Simba had a worried frown. 'Not properly, Bwana.'

'*Kumbe*,' said Daudi, 'he means this – you go to live at Makali. Build your house, and live in God's way in this devil's village, and slowly build the work so that a teacher may come and…'

'But, Bwana, this has nothing to do with Perisi.'

'Hasn't it though? What is her work?'

'Bwana, she is a teacher… *Heeh!* I see it.' He threw up his hands and rolled his eyes. '*Kah*, it is a way of wisdom truly.'

'Build your house, be a hunter; trap leopards and snakes, sell their skins to buy cows for your dowry. But live the life of a Christian; tell the stories of the people who lost their sickness at the hospital.'

'*Hongo*, Bwana, I see it. The children will come to see my skins, and to eat of the meat I kill as a hunter. I will tell them stories of hunting and animals and stories of God.'

'That's it – and live your life in God's way. Watch your words, your doings and your thoughts. Remember, when you fought the lion you did so alone, but in this fight you have God as your leader.'

Daudi turned over the pages of the Chigogo New Testament. 'Here are the words, Simba. "I can do everything through him who gives me strength." Take these words and prove yourself His man.'

Simba picked up his spear and his *cifuko* – a sort of calico bag in which were all his belongings.

'*Kwaheri*, I will go now, Bwana. *Yoh!*'

'*Kumbe*,' said Daudi 'will you not wait another day and plan?'

Simba shook his head. 'I go now. There is little time and –' He put his hand on his chest and grinned.

'Come to the hospital, Simba,' I said, 'I will give you eyedrops and pills to stop pain. They may be useful.'

Soon a bottle of aspirin and another of black eyedrops were stowed away in Simba's *cifuko*.

'Bwana,' he said, as we shook hands African fashion, 'behold, tell Perisi that the seed is planted, but that it needs watering.' He stepped out along the path resolutely.

'He means, Bwana, that he wants her prayers,' said Daudi in a low tone.

7

Sticking Plaster

Daudi dropped his tone to a mere whisper. 'Bwana, there is a man who has come all the way from the village of Makali, where Simba has started his work. Here is his first case. Behold, Bwana, this man, Moto, is a sub-chief and very important. I'll carry on with the out-patients while you go and see him. He is standing outside your office. It will be a very good thing if we can save him some trouble. Behold, this will help Simba in his new work.'

I nodded and handed my stethoscope to Daudi.

'You carry on then. I'll be back soon.'

In front of my office stood a tall African whose face was lined with obvious suffering.

'Mbukwa,' I said, holding out both my hands in the African greeting. He took them and then told me a story which I had heard scores of times. The story of a man working in his garden and bruising his shin with the hoe. The bruise had become a sore, the sore an ulcer. Only too well I knew what followed although he didn't tell me – the witch-doctor with his various poultices, largely made from cow manure, the ulcer spreading all the time, and sometimes becoming intensely painful. This is what had happened to the man who stood before me.

'*Kah*, Bwana,' he said, 'behold it pains me to walk. It pains me to sit. It pains me to lie. Day and night it throbs and aches. *Kah*, Bwana there is no joy in living with an *ilonda*, an ulcer. Have you medicine that will help? Simba says that ulcers are only a small affair at this hospital.'

'Truly, Great One, we have strong medicine for ulcers. Come into the room where we deal with them.'

He followed me into a dressing-room, its table piled with bandages and ointment. Kefa was making things tidy after a busy morning. I gave him instructions to bathe the leg and clean it up and to call me when all was ready. That ulcer was an ugly sight.

'*Kah*,' said the dresser. 'Phew, it is not a good thing; neither food for the eyes nor yet the nose.'

'*Heeh*,' said the sub-chief, 'Bwana, do I not know? Is it not on my leg?'

I went into the dispensary and mixed up a powder. I brought it back, and told the chief to put out his tongue. He was given a gourd of water and drank down the pain-relieving medicine, making wry faces as he did so.

'*Yah*, Bwana, *heeh*, what medicine. *Kah!* It has the bitterness of salt.'

'That,' I said, 'will stop your pain, and now for the ulcer.'

Carefully I put a dressing over the area, which was as big as the palm of your hand. Going to a special cupboard, of which I kept the key, I took out a roll of elastic sticking plaster. I could have used a hundred-weight of this every year, but I had only three spools in the whole hospital. I turned to the sub-chief.

'Listen. This is a very special type of bandage. It stays in its place all by itself. It keeps away the insects. It stops the skin from getting itchy. You can leave it covering your ulcer for three weeks, and, behold, in that time there will be much healing. But, you must not take it off!'

'*Hoh*,' said the African, 'but how will I know what is going on? How will I know it's getting better?'

'You must take my word for that. Have I not seen very many people with this sort of trouble?'

Moto nodded his head. But he was not convinced. Soon I saw him walking home clutching a dozen aspirin tablets tied carefully in the corner of the cloth that he wore around his middle.

'*Heh*,' said Kefa, 'behold, Bwana, here is a man who will not follow out what he is told. Mark my words.'

As it proved, Kefa's statement was only too true.

It was a week later. Again I was doing out-patients. This time Daudi came with a broad smile on his face.

'Bwana,' he said, 'it's a good thing there are two doors to this room. Behold, outside that door (he pointed with his chin) is the man on whose leg you put the elastic plaster. And outside that door (he pointed in the opposite direction) is Simba. Bwana, Simba has a smile so big that it must hurt his mouth, and, Bwana, he has laughed until his ribs are sore. He wants to talk to you.'

I went outside and there was Simba looking as though he had a story to tell which would not keep. After going through the usual greetings he said:

'Bwana, my stomach aches with laughter when I even think of Moto. I told him stories of how you healed ulcers. He came back and he said that all my words were true. Behold, you had given him medicine. *Heeh!*' – he wrinkled his face – 'medicine that stopped the pain. You then painted on medicine of a very strong colour, and then covered it with the cloth that stays in place all by itself. Bwana, he was full of your praise for four days, and then, behold, he decided that he must see how the ulcer was getting on.'

I looked at Daudi and smiled. This had happened before.

'Then, Bwana,' continued Simba, 'he tried to lift the plaster aside that he might see, but, behold, it had strength and would not move. And then he took hold of the end of it and pulled. It came off very well, but, Bwana, it stuck together. He tried to undo it. Behold, it was very strongly stuck, and his hands are not the hands of skill. Soon he saw that he had ruined your very special bandage, so he decided that he would take it right off. But, Bwana, the bandage was stuck to the hairs of his leg. *Heeh*,' Simba laughed, 'You should have heard it. *"Yah, Yah, Yah!"* he cried as the hairs came off.'

'Come,' I said, 'be a man, pull it off. You're a strong man making a noise like a child of the village.'

'He pulled it suddenly, strongly. *Yah*, and Bwana, did he yell! And then he sat there groaning. The ulcer looked very much as it had always looked.

'*Kah*' he said, 'the medicine of the Bwana does not work.'

'Behold,' I said, 'do you follow the words of the witchdoctor? Do you take a charm from round your neck after you have worn it for four days, or do you leave it there?'

'*Kah*,' he said, 'I leave it there.'

'Right,' said I, 'and why do you take the Bwana's special cloth off your leg?'

'Behold, I wanted to see what was happening to the ulcer.'

'Did the Bwana not say that you should not do so?'

'The Bwana said so, but, behold, I wanted to see.'

'*Hongo!*' I said, 'and if your ulcer goes very wrong now, is it the effect of your work or the medicine of the Bwana?'

'*Heeh*, Bwana, I talked to him with strong words. Behold, he is here.'

It so happened that that very day I had been sent a parcel which was wrapped inside with cellophane. I had been thinking how to conserve my supplies of sticking plaster, and I had brought some of this cellophane to the hospital, and sterilised it. It seemed to me that here was just one of the cases that I required, to try it out. First I listened to a long story from Moto, which was not particularly truthful, although it was very dramatic.

When he had finished I said, 'Behold, and when you pulled the cloth off, was the pain any better?'

'Bwana,' he said, 'there was no pain.'

'Oh,' I said, taking a couple of hairs on his leg and pulling them.

'*Yah*,' he said, 'that hurts. Of course it hurts.'

'*Koh*? and did it not hurt when the bandage pulled out your hairs?'

'Bwana, I – er – well, you see – I – er –'

He looked confused. I looked at him and grinned. 'Now if I do more treatment you must promise to follow my words. If you disobey, then no more treatment.'

'Bwana, I will follow your words.'

'Right,' I said.

Taking some of the cellophane I covered the ulcer.

'You can see through that, can't you?' I said. 'You can see the ulcer?'

'*Heeh*, Bwana!' he nodded.

Above and below the plastic material I put the elastic strapping. The African chief looked at it in amazement.

'*Kah*,' he said, 'that's wisdom. I can see the ulcer. I can see the medicine, and yet, the *dudus*, insects, can't get into it.'

'Right,' I said, 'now come back and see me in three weeks.'

He nodded. I went out of the room and there was Simba. I took him aside.

'Did you see what happened? When Moto did not follow out my words he got into trouble.'

'*Heeh*, and Bwana, did he get into trouble!'

The African rubbed his eyes.

'Simba,' I said, 'that will happen to you. It will happen to you and to me and to everyone of us if we do not obey the words of God.'

Simba nodded slowly.

'Listen, my friend. I will give you the words that Jesus Himself spoke to a young man who came to Him and asked how he could get the life that never ends, the life that is all joy, the life that is never easy, but always worthwhile. "Behold," He said, "you must love the Lord your God with all your heart and with all your soul and with all your mind and with all your strength."'

Simba nodded again. 'Bwana, I read that the other day, and then Jesus said, "You must love the other man as much as you love yourself."'

'Truly, those are God's instruction to His own children. And they are true of the village of Makali. Behold, not only will you do work for God there, but if you seek first His will, His Kingdom, then all the other things that you desire will come your way if they are in His plan.'

'*Kumbe*, Bwana,' said Simba, 'I see it. It is better to trust God than to get impatient and start pulling off the plaster to see what is happening.'

He moved towards the gate. I put my hand on his bare shoulder.

'Remember, Lion-hunter, if God wants things to go faster He will make things happen that way.'

8

Despair and Disease

Sechelela put the baby back in its cot and pointed with her chin towards the scales where the children were weighed.

'There is a letter for you there. It was brought this morning from the school.'

I tore open the envelope which was addressed in very good handwriting. I read it for a moment, then turned round to her and smiled.

'Sechie, this is from Perisi.'

'*Kumbe*,' said the old African matron, 'what are her words, Bwana?'

'She says that she would like to come to the hospital to train as a nurse, so that she may learn the ways of babies.'

Sechelela nodded her head. 'Bwana, I have seen this coming for many days. Behold, Perisi is a girl of wisdom and her thoughts are good thoughts. She has been at the school for many years. I remember how her father thought she would die in the days after her mother's death. Behold, was not his wife my friend? He gave the child into my arms, so I brought her to the school.'

'How old was she then, Sechie?'

'*Eeh!* About five, Bwana. Did she not have much malaria? So we gave her quinine medicine, and her fever was conquered. Her father went on a great safari to the coast, and left her behind. Was she not fed and clothed and taught at the school? But, Bwana, these days when she is of marriageable age her father has returned. He demands that she should return to him from the school and if she goes back to his house her life will be spoilt.'

'*Hongo*, he must be a nasty character.'

She nodded vigorously. '*Kumbe*, he is a man of great greed, and he cares only for money, so that he may buy the things for which he has great appetite. Behold, there will be a great *shauri*, discussion, about this soon. Bwana, if she comes to the hospital it will be much safer for her. Am I not here to see that no harm comes to her?'

Late that afternoon I interviewed Perisi. 'Bwana,' she said, 'I wish to come and learn the words and wisdom of the hospital. Behold, am I not a teacher, have I not my certificate? Therefore I can learn very quickly. Since I can read English I can understand the books that are not readable by those who only know the African languages.'

'Have you no other reason, Perisi?'

She looked me fairly between the eyes. 'Bwana, I have other reasons. My father would have me marry a man who is *mushenzishenzi,* as heathen as can be, a man with three other wives. *Kah*, Bwana, in being his wife there would be no joy. But he has seen my father, and they have agreed to a dowry of twenty-eight cows, and twenty goats. Bwana, you know my father's way.' She shrugged her shoulders.

'But, Perisi, if you stay with us in hospital here for a year, and learn the ways of babies and mothers, well, what then?'

'*Kah*, Bwana,' said the African girl, 'it may be that during that time someone else will come along. Someone who will offer my father the same sort of dowry, and at the same time be a person whose wife I could be with joy.' She looked down at the ground and started to push a pebble round with her toes.

'Perisi,' I said quietly, 'it says in God's Book that the ways of a good man are ordered by the Lord.'

'Behold, Bwana,' said Perisi, eagerly interrupting. 'Bwana, that is my prayer, that my life may be according to His plan, that I may obey Him, and then, Bwana, I will be useful in life and in being useful and going His way, life will be full and happy and worth living.'

'Very well, then,' I said, 'I'll go and talk to the people at the school, and at the end of this term, if they agree, you will come to the hospital and learn the things that we have to teach.'

I was bidding her goodbye at the hospital gates when a lean athletic African came running along the path with a letter for me held in a split stick. In a very wobbling hand was written:

Bwana, I am following with three children, one is burnt and is very sick and the other two are not so sick.

The signature was Simba's.

I made what preparation I could. Just after sunset they arrived. One child was in a hammock. The other, a pathetic little chap, with a broken arm, was carried pick-a-back fashion by his mother, while a twelve-year-old girl followed behind the others. In the middle of her back was a great lump as big as her head.

As we undid the hammock Simba said to me:

'Bwana, I have collected the children of Makali who are ill, and brought them to you. Behold this child' (I held a hurricane lantern where I could see a wasted little person, who lay with staring eyes on the crude blanket that had been used as the stretcher) 'this child, Bwana, was knocked into the fire by her grandfather when he was drunk. Behold, Bwana, she is much burnt.'

I stooped to examine her. The little girl let out a feeble scream. The big hunter was down on his knees.

'*Ulece kogopa mwendece,* don't be frightened, little one, the Bwana will not bring pain, he takes it away.'

I had a loaded syringe in my hand. A minute later the little child had a pain-controlling drug active within her small body. She had a horrible burn.

'Simba,' I said, 'there's only one thing for this child, as there was only one thing for you when you came in – a blood transfusion. Will you talk to her relations and fix it up for me? While that is being arranged I will treat the others.'

The little boy with the broken collar-bone was in intense pain also. The witch-doctor's activity had done much to cause a tremendous swelling, but a whiff of anaesthetic and the bone was in place. Then with some sticking plaster and a sling the child was soon comfortable.

The child with the lump on her back was intensely sensitive about it. In a matter of five minutes it was clear to me that a simple operation would rid her for ever of what she called her burden.

The parents of the child with the burn were engaged in a very wordy and noisy conference which Simba seemed to be chairing in the out-patients' department. I went across to them.

'Listen,' I said, 'we must start this transfusion quickly if the life of the little one is to be saved.'

Simba shook his head. 'Bwana, I have spoken many words. I have told them that this is a way of wisdom and a way of life, but they will not listen. They say it shall not be done. They want other medicine, not this. Will you not put on the medicine that you put on the Chief's ulcer, that the skin may heal?'

I did my best to explain to them that there was more to a burn than putting ointments and bandages on it. But they would take no notice of what I had to say, or for that matter, what anybody else had to say.

'No,' they said, 'we will only allow medicine to be put on the burn.'

I did what I could in this direction. It was nearly midnight by the time I had completed treatment. The child was asleep, but I knew that all was far from well.

I took Simba aside. 'My friend, this is not the way that the child should be treated. This is not the medicine that brings life. All we are doing is covering up the wound; we are not curing the root of the trouble. The child's relations are like those who would sit and cover their sins by putting on clean clothes, or a bright smile. This is not enough. Did not Jesus say, "No man comes to the Father, but by Me?"'

Simba nodded. '*Heeh*, Bwana, with your knowledge of the trouble you say that a blood transfusion is the only way?'

'Truly, Simba, there is no other.'

We went back into the ward together. I looked at the child, felt her pulse. There was nothing else for it. I went out to see the relations.

'Listen,' I said, 'there are those who will give the child what she needs – this is the only way – without it the child cannot live. Another hour's delay and she will die.'

They shook their heads.

Simba tapped my elbow. 'Bwana, I will give the blood.'

'Hear my words,' I said, 'Simba will give his blood that the child may live. He wants no money, no cows, nothing!'

The father stood up. 'Bwana, we refuse. The words are finished.'

At dawn I was awakened by the terrifying noise that an African makes when someone has died. Simba came running down to my doorstep.

'Bwana,' he said, 'before the sun appeared the child died. The people have run away taking her with them, and, Bwana, worse still, they have taken the child with the broken arm and the girl with the burden on her back. Bwana, this is failure. There will be only anger waiting for me in the village of Malaki.'

Simba sat under the shade of a baobab tree just outside the hospital gate. His eyes were closed and his teeth chattered noisily. I came over to him and put my hand on his shoulder. His skin seemed on fire.

'Simba,' I said. He started to his feet.

'Bwana, where – eh...'

'You're sick, old man. You'd better come into the hospital and I'll give you some medicine.'

'Bwana, I didn't sleep last night, Behold, my head throbs and throbs and throbs. *Heeh*, my heart has no bottom to it. Behold, all my work is *bwete*, worthless. How I have tried to be useful, but…'

He put his head in his hands and groaned. His whole body shook with a shivering attack. I took his arm and helped him over to the hospital. He looked in the direction of the school and said in a husky voice:

'Bwana, I have not succeeded in my work for God, and how can I prove then to Perisi that I am worthy of her? *Kah*, Bwana, it would have been better if you had never saved my life in the hospital there.'

'*Hongo*, my friend,' I said, 'it is never wise to make decisions when you're angry or when you're sick. Into bed with you, take medicine, sleep for some hours, eat, and then we will talk again of these things.'

I saw them tuck Simba under four blankets and I injected quinine into the large muscles of his thigh.

'*Heeh*,' said Simba, as the needle came out. '*Kah*, Bwana, behold that needle feels like a spear.'

'It is a spear,' I replied, 'and it has on its point the medicine that is poison to *dudus* of malaria. Behold, even at this moment they are fleeing from the medicine, but they will be caught as surely as you catch the snakes that you hunt.'

Daudi appeared on the scene with two aspirin tablets, and a gourd full of water. The pills were put on Simba's tongue and he swallowed them.

He cleared his throat with his famous imitation of a lion's roar. '*Kah*, Bwana, that's medicine. It takes the pain from your head and the pain from your muscles. *Yah,*' he stretched comfortably, 'the C.M.S. Hospital is the place of relief of great pain. *Yah*. But I'm cold.'

Daudi put the thermometer under his arm; held it there carefully then he took it out and read it:

'A hundred and three point four, Bwana.'

As he was about to shake it down Simba asked, 'Bwana, what are the words of the glass nail?'

'The what?'

Daudi smiled. 'Bwana, he wants to know what his temperature is. The glass nail is the thermometer.'

'*Hoh*,' I said, 'the words of the glass nail are these, that you will stay in bed for perhaps three days, then you will feel better.'

'But, Bwana, does it say that I must have your little spear stuck into me again?'

I nodded. 'It calls for the spear at least three times more.'

'*Yah*,' said Simba, and pulled the blankets tightly round him.

At that moment a strident voice came through the window.

'*Kah*,' it said, 'these *Wazungu*, Europeans, *heeh*, behold they are people of...' There was the sound of someone spitting.

I looked at Daudi and raised my eyebrows and grinned.

85

'Bwana,' he whispered, 'it would be good to listen a little longer.'

The voice was going on. 'Behold, for many years they have kept my daughter from me, and now, behold, when it comes to the matter of her marriage, they are making trouble. But I, Mafuta, will show them my great strength, and they will flee as does the hyena when the lion appears.'

Daudi grinned very widely. 'Bwana,' he whispered, 'this is the father of Perisi.'

When he heard the girl's name, Simba lifted his head.

'*Heh*,' he said, 'what?'

'Lie quietly,' I said, 'behold, Perisi's father has arrived. It would sound to me as though he had been drinking much *wujimbi*, beer.'

'Lie still, Simba. Listen to these words, and, behold, learn from them.'

I went out of the door. '*Mbukwa*,' I said.

'*Kah*,' said the African who, I discovered, was called *Mafuta*, oil, because he was so fat.

He rolled his bloodshot eyes but said nothing.

'Behold,' I said, 'Mbisi, the hyena, has come to flee from the anger and words of Nhembo, the elephant.'

The dressers giggled, and Mafuta looked uncomfortable.

'*Yah*,' said Daudi, 'not Nhembo, the elephant. Surely he is Ngubi, the wart hog.'

The situation did not look particularly promising. A group of old men convalescing squatted under a pomegranate bush, so I motioned to them all to sit in the shade. I lifted my hand.

'Behold, let me state my case, O Great Ones of the tribe. Will you hear the *shauri* between this man of great girth and myself?'

The tension was at once eased. The fat African sat down and I started with my tale.

'*Katali,* long ago, there was a man who lived in this country of Wagogo, and, behold, his one possession was a calf; a calf without much strength whose legs wobbled when she walked. The man had no way of feeding his calf, and he found no joy in being a herdsman. One day he said, "Behold, I will go to

another country and see if there my fortunes will improve." So he went away from his house. And his neighbours found the calf walking in the jungle, and they took it to be in their own herd. Behold, they fed it, and gave it healing leaves and herbs. It grew to become a creature of strength. In the time of drought water was carried for it. In the days when there was no grass to be found it was fed with grain from the store of those who were his neighbours.

'Harvest after harvest passed. The calf had become a cow. Perhaps the best cow in the whole herd. One day the traveller came back from his great safari. He came to his house.

'He said to those who lived near him, "Return to me my calf." So they said to him, "Which calf?"

'"Why," he said, "the one that I left behind."

'"*Yah*," said his neighbours, "behold, your calf was sick, you left it to die, and behold, we fed it with our flocks. We watered it with our herds; while you rested in the shade we carried water from the wells to give it drink; while you sat in the places near the sea and ate mangoes we took it out to the grazing."

'Behold' I turned to the group of old African men who were sitting crouched up in the shade. 'Tell me, Great Ones, who owned that calf? The man who went on the journey or the people who looked after the cow? Give me your judgment.'

For a while the old men talked in whispers, their heads close together, then one of them, leaning on his spear, said, 'Bwana, the calf belonged to the man who went on the journey, but behold, he could not have it back until he paid his neighbours the price of its food, and should he not also make a gift to those who looked after it?'

'*Heeh*,' said 'Daudi, 'those are words of wisdom, Great Ones.'

Turning to Mafuta, who was almost snarling, he said: 'Behold, your daughter Perisi was sick, and likely to die. You left her alone in your house. She was taken by the *Wabibi*, the ladies of the C.M.S. school, medicine was given to her, she was fed and taught, and now when she reaches the age when she can marry, behold, you come to collect the cows of her dowry.'

Mafuta struggled to his feet, stuttering with rage.

'*Kah*,' he said, 'I'll –' But exactly what he was going to do was lost in one enormous hiccough.

I could hear a noise within the ward. Simba was struggling out from beneath his blankets.

'Bwana,' he said, 'I must speak to him, behold, I must arrange this matter. Hee... Bwana,' his eyes flashed with anger and with the fever that was raging in his body, 'I could beat him with a stick, a knobbed stick, until he cried.'

'Lie down, my friend,' I said. 'Behold, there is no need to do those things. Mafuta has great anger. No good will be done by matching it with your more fierce anger. Listen, I will read to you from God's Book.'

I turned over the pages of the Chigogo New Testament.

'"Happy are the meek people for they shall inherit the earth." Now Simba mark this, it says "meek" not "weak." A meek man is a strong one who controls himself. Behold, your way of winning this hunt is to tell

God of your problem, ask Him to show you the path, and when He does, follow it and obey His word. In that way you will get an answer. Follow your own way, the way of anger or the way of strife and there will be no joy for anyone. But follow the way of meekness, of control, of wisdom and all will come right. God does not speak idle words.'

Perspiration stood out on Simba's forehead. I tucked the blankets round him.

'*Assante!* Thank you, Bwana,' he said, 'that's better. *Kah*, your medicine is even now working. My pains are less, I can even now feel the cold hand of fever leaving me.' He paused and then: '*Hee...* I will follow the way of wisdom.'

A strange shuffling sound came from outside. I looked through the window. Stumbling along the path that led across to the native village went Mafuta, waving his fist in the air, and hiccoughing noisily as he went. I wondered just how the whole matter was going to work out.

9

Betrothal Drums

The moon was exceptionally bright. I looked at the plains through the mosquito wire of the ward window. Through the fine mesh the moon looked as though radiating from it was a cross. My eyes wandered beyond the close-up baobab tree to the fringe of thornbush where the jungle began. Far beyond this I could hear the wild throbbing of drums and the high-pitched singing of African voices. There was a hectic rhythm about the whole thing that night. My watch showed the time as ten minutes to two.

'Bwana,' said a husky voice from somewhere in the partial darkness beside me, 'when are you going to give me medicine?'

'Before long, Simba. Is not Daudi looking at your blood under the microscope so that we may see what is the right medicine to give?'

Again silence fell. In the shadows only a few yards away an animal walked silently past. Its outline looked vaguely like that of an Alsatian dog. At that moment I heard a voice beside me. I turned to see Simba wrapped in a blanket looking over my shoulder. '*Mbisi,* the hyena, Bwana. Would that I had my spear.' The animal disappeared in the thornbush. Simba touched my arm: 'Listen to the drums, Bwana, hear them.'

I nodded. 'I don't like the sound of it. What does it tell you, Simba?'

'Bwana, those are the drums of a betrothal. They come from the direction where Mafuta went yesterday. Behold, perhaps even now the matter is completed. The cows are paid over and Perisi is no longer free.' He shivered.

'*Kumbe!* Simba,' I said, 'you've been sick. You ought to be back in bed. It's no good for you getting up at this hour of the night thinking these thoughts.'

'*Kah*,' said he, 'Bwana, how can I sleep when I feel those drums pounding in my heart, and when I know, Bwana, that down there,' he pointed with his chin towards the school, 'the same is probably happening to Perisi. *Kumbe*, Bwana, let me take this thing into my hands. I will fight for her.'

'*Hee…*' I said, 'I know what you'd do. Look at the man down there, in the bed third from the end. Did he not do the same, did he not get a knife stuck into him? And behold, I have others here who have had spears through them, or into them, and then, behold, they spend some time in the *cidindilo* – where the door is locked, and where on one's clothes there is the mark of the arrow. Is this the way that you would show Perisi that you have turned from the ways of the heathen to follow the ways of God? Eh?'

'*E-e-e-e-h,* I don't know what to do, Bwana, I don't know what to do, but I must do something.'

'*Hongo*, Simba. Those are the words of those who wear charms about their necks and rub themselves with lion fat. They get joy from the work of rubbing. Their skin shines, but their pain remains. People such as these like to hear the witch-doctor muttering his charms, and throwing his shoes to see why the spirits have attacked people.'

Simba nodded slowly.

'It is more interesting to those of your tribe to see this than to see us take a drop of blood from a man's finger, look at it under a microscope, find the disease and then come with a syringe and inject the medicine that cures. But, *hongo*, our way works.'

'*Hee…*' grinned Simba, rubbing himself tenderly over the area of his hip pocket. 'Behold, Bwana, it works all right.'

'*Viswanu,*' I said, 'right, let us follow God's way in this larger matter of yours. If we pray, God hears, that is, if we are members of His family; have I not told you that many times? It is not enough to run to God and pray when you are in trouble or sick. God is not merely a strong Chief to whom we run if we are in danger or trouble. Rather God is a father to whom His children go, day by day, about all manner of things, big and small. God certainly will save you from danger or damage, but He does much more. He thinks of every step in your life, and He answers your prayers, unless something is wrong in the way you live. For instance, does not God's Book say, "If I have iniquity – plans for sin – in my heart, the Lord will not hear me?"'

'*Kah*, Bwana, but I have no plans for sin. I plan to do things for God.'

'That being so, Simba, this is what God says, "Commit your way unto the Lord, trust also in Him, and He will bring it to pass."'

'*Heh*,' said Simba, 'Bwana, that sounds just right.'

'Come on, then, let's kneel down here and commit your way to God.' And pray Simba did.

We had just got up from our knees when I heard the closing of the laboratory door. A minute later Daudi was with us.

'Bwana,' said he, 'the hunter has been hunted. Behold, all his blood slides are full of the *dudus* from the nose of Izuguni, the mosquito. *Kah!* He has very much malaria.'

The injection of quinine was duly given and Simba put to bed. Once again, I looked through the window, across the plain.

'*Heh*,' said Simba as he wrapped the blanket round his shoulder, 'I wish I knew, Bwana, how God was going to straighten this whole thing out. It looks impossible to me.'

He shook his head and then suddenly the rays of the moonlight, reflected in the cross-like fashion on the mosquito wire, caught his attention from where he lay.

'*Kah*, Bwana,' he said, 'look at that – right over the village where it is all happening. Behold it looks as though the Cross of the Lord is above it.'

'Simba,' I said, 'that's only a trick of the moonlight and fine wire, but believe me, God is there as He is here. You see when we pray, God sets to work.'

'*Heh*, Bwana,' said Simba, 'I will go back to sleep now, knowing that Almighty God is working.'

I had exactly the same feeling as I walked home across the plain.

Next morning we got news from the small boy who beats the drum.

'*Kah*, Bwana,' he said, 'in the village beyond the thornbush, they had a *sikuku* last night. *Hee*… Bwana! Much beer, much dancing, and this morning, many people with headaches. Also Bwana, I hear that Makaranga, the Chief there – *yoh*, he is a man of many wives – has given the betrothal gifts, and received betrothal gifts. Bwana, I hear that he has given Mafuta a ring made all from gold for his finger.'

The same news apparently had reached the hospital.

'Daudi,' I said, 'tell me, what about this ring? Is that a usual thing for a betrothal gift?'

'*Heh!* This is a new thing, Bwana.'

'Hmm, a gold ring, eh? Well, that can't lead to much trouble.' But little did I guess to how much!

Simba was lying in bed shivering. He was still under the grip of the malaria. I advanced upon him with a loaded syringe. 'Come on, old hunter,' I said, 'turn over. Behold, today I am the hunter, and you are the hunted.'

'*Yoh*, Bwana,' he said turning over, '*yoh*, anybody can stick a spear into a half-dead animal.'

I rubbed an area of skin as big as a shilling with a swab soaked in methylated spirit and stuck the needle in.

'*Hee*…' he gasped. '*Kah*, Bwana, I don't feel well this morning.'

'Oh,' I said, 'have you any hunger?'

There was a slight grin on his face.

Daudi behind me was smiling broadly. 'That is as well, Bwana, because some of the *wadodo waskooli*, the small girls from the school, have arrived with a dish of *wugali,* porridge, for Simba. Bwana, Perisi herself cooked it.'

Simba was sitting up in bed. '*Yah*, Bwana,' he said. '*Heh*… I have joy and I commence to feel better.'

'The thought of food did that to you, eh?'

'*Heh*, Bwana, you would laugh at me, but my thoughts are a little higher than my stomach. They're in my heart. Behold, does Perisi not think of my sickness? Is she not a woman of great capacity?'

I went outside the ward. Not far away was the subject of our conversation.

'Bwana,' she said, 'my work at the hospital will start soon?'

'You've started already, Perisi, for you've done a lot of good to one of my patients this morning.'

The African girl smiled and then her face became very serious.

'Bwana, I could not sleep last night. I heard those drums.'

'We heard them too up here. We asked God to make this whole matter go His way.'

'Bwana, I too prayed like that, but I don't see how it can happen.'

'That isn't your job, Perisi, or mine. Your job is to pray and obey any order. God does the work, and if He has anything for us to do in the matter He shows it.'

'*Mbeka, Mbeka*, truly', she said nodding.

At that moment Daudi arrived with the empty porridge pot. Perisi took it up, bade us good morning, and went back to the school.

'*Heh*, Bwana,' said Daudi, 'behold, is it not an unusual thing in our tribe for men and women to love one another as those two do?'

10

Dowries and Doings

There was an hysterical note in the voice. 'I must see the Bwana. I must see the Bwana now.'

Then came a quiet murmur that I could not sift out into words, and once again the high-pitched voice. 'He's drinking his tea, is he? *Kah!* As though his tea meant anything to me. Behold, am I not in danger? Am I not in pain? Am I not in trouble? I must have the Bwana, now, now, now!' The voice rose to a scream.

I recognised the quiet tones of Daudi's voice. 'Ooh,' he said, 'go and visit the witch-doctor – that's what everyone in the tribe does if a spell has been cast.'

'*Hongo!*' came the voice. 'Should I visit the witch-doctor when a spell has been cast for one of the richest men in all the country?'

Daudi laughed scornfully and wagged his finger. 'Also, if you went to the witch-doctor he would charge you a cow…'

I walked out of the door at this moment, and was almost knocked down by Mafuta, who came rushing at me. He waved his podgy hand,

'Gently,' I said, '*heh, pole, pole* – what's it all about?'

'Bwana, look at my hand.'

The second finger was swollen and sausage-like, and looked extremely uncomfortable. Mafuta was almost spluttering in his eagerness to tell me about it. 'Bwana,' he said, 'behold, I – I – I – I…' He seemed suddenly to realise that he was getting himself into deep water.

'Oh,' I said, 'yes, I heard about it. You were given a gold ring by Makaranga – the gift of a rich Chief, eh. Let's have a look at this ring. Where is it?'

'It's there, Bwana, it's there.'

'Where?' I asked frowning.

'Under there.'

He jabbed at me with his swollen finger. Holding his hand I turned it this way and that but I could see nothing. The ring was completely hidden by swollen flesh. I examined the finger carefully. Daudi pointed out the whitish area beneath the nail.

'Bwana,' he said, 'behold, it has a peculiar colour today.'

I looked up at the African's eyes. They too were a strange yellow colour. 'Put out your tongue,' I ordered.

'*H-e-e-e…*' said Daudi, shuddering, 'put it back.'

I agreed with him that it was not a pretty sight.

'Bwana,' said the dispenser in English, 'he has been drinking much beer.'

'Also, his liver is in trouble. Behold, is he not jaundiced?'

I turned my attention to the fat man's feet. They too were swollen. I pushed my thumb into the skin over his shin bone. When I did this a big dimple remained.

'Sit in the shade here,' I ordered, 'and keep your hand in cold water for two hours. Drink also the medicine that I will give you. Then, behold, I will help you and remove from your finger the gift of your friend, the very rich Chief.'

'*Heh*,' said Mafuta, 'he is not my friend, Bwana. Behold, it was he who cast the spell against me. Bwana, he would kill me.'

A deep and very unpleasant rumbling sound came from somewhere within his massive interior. '*Yeh*, Bwana, see how he wishes me evil.'

Daudi looked at me with wide-open eyes. 'Bwana,' he said, 'it is not a good thing for a man to talk like this about someone who is betrothed to his daughter. Behold, it looks –' He lifted his eyebrows expressively.

'Doesn't it?' I replied. 'Now whatever you do, keep Simba away from him.'

This did not prove a hard problem since I saw Simba in the little grass-roofed hut in which the drums were kept. He was sitting on a three-legged stool with his head in his hands. I went across.

'*Ati za hako*? What is the news?'

101

'Bwana,' said Simba slowly lifting his head, 'I have great doubts. There are strong spells being cast in this matter. The hand of Shaitan, the devil, is obvious in our country these days. His hand is active against me. Everything is going wrong.'

'*Heh*,' I said, 'I know what you need. It is not a medicine for your body or for your mind; it's an injection for your soul. Listen, since the days of your fight with the lion have you not become a son of God?'

Simba nodded.

'Have you not followed out the words of God Himself when he said, "To those who trust in His Name He has given the privilege of becoming children of God"? Where's your trust, man?'

'*Heh*,' said Simba, 'who am I to trust, Bwana? How am I to know that God can do this thing?'

'*Heeh,*' I said, 'now you sit down there and listen. Here is an incident from God's own Book, in which we see what Jesus can do to Shaitani – and for those who fight on his side. Jesus and His followers had crossed a lake, and arriving on the other side, the minute they put their feet on the ground, there rushed towards them a fierce-looking man whose wild-looking eyes told the story of a mind unbalanced.'

Simba shivered. '*Kah…* Bwana, I know that look.'

'Truly, and the followers of the Lord Jesus felt as you do, because this man was so strong that no one in the country could bind or hold him. He broke chains, he tore ropes into little pieces. There he wandered, day and night, climbing over rough rocks, lingering in the place of burial of his ancestors, shrieking wildly and gashing himself with sharp stones.

'When he saw Jesus in the distance he rushed along the side of the lake, then suddenly threw himself at Jesus' feet, and cried out in a loud, frightened voice, "What do you want with me, Jesus, Son of God" – and then more softly – "In God's Name I beg of you do not torment me" – for Jesus had spoken and said "*Icisi,* evil spirit, come out of the man." And then Jesus went on talking.

'"What is your name?" He asked. It was the evil spirit that replied. "*Wenji,* very many, for there are a host of us."

'But listen, Simba, here is the thing for you. The spirits begged Jesus not to send them away out of the country where they were. They knew that Jesus had power over them. They knew that God is stronger than Satan, and so they begged of Him that He would

103

not send them away, but into a great herd of pigs that were on the slope of a hill. Jesus did so, but the man, who a little while before had been wild and dangerous, was calm. His eyes, too, were calm. He said to Jesus, "Let me come with you, Bwana." But Jesus said, "No, you go back to your own people and tell them what Almighty God has done for you."

'He did that, and everyone was astonished.

'Now, Simba, if you are confident and trust in Jesus, behold you will find that the hand of God is very much stronger than the hand of evil. Behold, God is very strong.'

'*Kah*,' said Simba, 'I have made a bad mistake, Bwana. I will speak to God and tell Him that I trust Him.'

'Right,' I said, 'now you pray like anything and keep out of this fight for the time being. When the time comes for fighting, fight you shall.'

Late that evening I went back to the ward. Mafuta was sitting up in bed. His finger was less swollen. I could just see the gold ring underneath the swollen flesh. I injected some local anæsthetic round the spot, and set to work with a hacksaw blade, two pairs of dental forceps, and a pocket-knife. It was not an easy operation, nor was it made easier by Mafuta who let out an elaborate series of groans and grunts.

'*Yah*, Bwana,' he said, 'be careful with that sharp thing,' as I picked up the pocket-knife. Then when I picked up the dental forceps gently to bend the gold after having cut through it, he let out a tremendous yell, saying that I would most surely pinch him, but when the ring was safely off he breathed a sigh of relief, and before I could stop him, grasped my hand, and kissed it, making a far from pleasant noise with his lips.

Daudi rocked with laughter. '*Heh*, Bwana,' he said, 'what a man is Mafuta here.'

I turned to the fat African who was tenderly rubbing his finger: 'Was it easy to put that ring on your finger?'

'*H-e-e-e*, Bwana,' he nodded vigorously.

'Was it easy to get off?'

'*Kumbe*, no Bwana, it was a thing of much danger and pain.'

'Did it give you joy to put it on?'

'*H-e-e-e*, Bwana-' Again he nodded.

'Behold, is not that ring like sin? It looked attractive – it was easy to get on your finger. Sin always looks attractive and easy. It requires neither brains nor courage to do it. But do not forget, it took the love of God, the courage and the understanding and the tremendous love of His Son to get rid of the punishment for sin, and the power of it.'

'Truly, Bwana, truly these are great words,' said the fat African, his eyes moving shiftily.

'*Yoh*,' said Daudi, 'Bwana, it is like pouring water on to hot earth, telling him the words of God. It just disappears. *Tichi!*' He threw up his hands expressively.

'No, Daudi, they stick in somewhere.'

'They haven't stuck far with him, Bwana, listen...'

Mafuta was muttering: '*Kah*, I will make trouble. I will make trouble for this one who would be the husband of my daughter. He cannot cast spells upon me without reaping trouble.'

There was a mosquito buzzing altogether too close to my ear. I woke up, switched on a torch, and found that the insect was on the outside of the net a few inches away from my head, making valiant efforts to get through the fine mesh. I glanced at my watch – 2 a.m. Even as I put out the torch I could hear the sound of running feet coming from the direction of the hospital. Trouble, I thought, and expected the usual cry of 'Bwana, quickly, another baby.' But it was Daudi's voice:

'Bwana,' he said, 'quickly, Mafuta is screaming and yelling. He says that he is greatly bewitched and that he is about to die. He lies on the floor, Bwana, with his hands clasped over his middle, saying "*Yoh!*" There is froth at his mouth.'

By this time I was struggling into some clothes. Clasping a torch in one hand, I raced with Daudi to the hospital. The ungainly form of Mafuta lay on the floor. He was groaning and saying, '*O-o-o-o-h, y-a-a-a-a-a-a…. Yah! Yah! Kah, kah, kah.*' Then his voice would lift into a high-pitched scream like a circular saw hitting a nail.

He was a very difficult patient to examine since he was rolling all over the place. By the light of the hurricane lantern I could see that his eyes were nearly yellow, and it soon was abundantly clear that his gall bladder was playing him false. In less than a minute I had a syringe loaded with two particular drugs and I injected them into him as he lay on the floor groaning.

I explained to Daudi what was the cause of the whole thing. Mafuta didn't seem to be listening.

'Behold,' I said, 'there is a little tube-like passage that comes from the gall bladder into your inside, your digestive tract –'

'Digestive tract?' said Daudi, 'Bwana, you mean the road along which the food passes.'

'Yes,' I said, 'I do, exactly that. Well, into this narrow tube, sometimes passes a little round stone which is made when the body has a problem with fat. If it is small, it may pass and give little pain, but if it is largish, it blocks up the tube, you go all yellow, and *heeh*, do you get pain? So you give the medicine through the needle to reduce the pain and to make that tube become loose, then the stone will slip through and the patient feels much better.'

Mafuta was mumbling: '*Kah… kah… ooh.*'

There was a glazed look in his eyes, and then in a strange voice like someone talking in their sleep he said, 'The feet of the witchdoctor, the feet of the witchdoctor are walking, walking round my house.'

He drew up his knees and started to groan. '*Ooi, ooi, Yah*ay, *Yah, Yah, Yah. Koh!* Does he not stamp with his feet upon the ground in front of my door! *Koh!* It is a spell, a spell that will kill me, will kill me.'

He seemed to become frenzied again. He leapt off the bed and fell on the floor with a horrid bump, and then with a groan he became unconscious. I had a bad five minutes trying to get him round. Twice I injected and then I saw his eyelids flicker, and his pulse felt a little more like a pulse. We got him back to bed – he lay there gasping. I took Daudi aside:

'What we must remember is that his heart is also weak – anything could happen to him.'

At that moment the door flew open. In rushed one of his cronies, taking no notice of us.

'*Yayagwe*, Oh, my mother,' he yelled, wringing his hands. '*Yayagwe*, there is great trouble. Behold, Makaranga, the chief has great anger towards you, and I saw Mganga, the witch-doctor, slip quietly into his house. *Heeh*, are we not in trouble?'

I expected my fat African patient to collapse under this news, and I prepared to meet the emergency, but instead of fear and collapse he sat up and roared like a bull.

'*Kah*,' said he, 'my daughter Perisi will never see the inside of his house. I am the one who should have anger. Was it not his ring on my finger which caused me much trouble? She shall marry another and he shall bear the brunt of this fight.'

I turned to Daudi who was sterilising a syringe that we had just used. 'Bwana,' he whispered, 'this is a change in the road his mind travels.'

'It is indeed, go and get Simba quickly. He's in the drum house.'

Soon the African hunter stood in the doorway with Daudi beside him.

Daudi sidled over to me. 'Bwana, I have explained the situation to him. You had better leave it now to us. We know how these things should be arranged.'

Nodding I moved over into a corner.

'*Mbukwa*, Good day,' said Simba.

Mafuta looked at him from his bed. '*Mbukwa*,' he replied, a cunning gleam coming into his eye. Simba turned to me:

'Bwana, since taking your medicine, I have regained my strength. Behold, it is time that I went hunting again. Behold, I will become a rich man if I continue to catch leopards and pythons as I have been doing. There is these days a great sale for their skins.'

Mafuta sat up in bed. He looked distinctly interested when it came to a matter of money. Daudi was whispering again into my ear:

'Bwana, you take Simba outside and I will do the negotiations. That is the way we do it in our tribe. Do not go far away, and behold, I will tell you what happens.'

This is what he told me a few minutes later. 'Bwana, old Mafuta is very keen that this matter should be fixed, and fixed at once. So I said to him, "What better husband could Perisi have than a hunter who could defend her, and in defending her, would defend her father?" Also here was one who could pay the full dowry of thirty cows, and Bwana, he has agreed.'

Simba grasped Daudi by the shoulder. 'What?' he almost shouted, 'Say it again.'

'I will,' said the dispenser, drawing back, 'if you stop hurting my shoulder. *Kah*, man, you're strong.'

The whole thing was gone over again slowly. Then Simba turned to me and said, 'Bwana, truly this is nothing but the hand of God. This morning there was no hope, everything seemed quite impossible. Now Bwana, it's happened.'

'Truly,' I said, 'but there's a fight in the air. This Makaranga is not going to be easy. And I truly believe, that these witch-doctor people will have every assistance that the devil can give them, for the simple reason that you are trying to serve God, and if the devil can upset God's work in any way, he'll do it.'

'*Heeh*,' said Simba, 'today, and to date, *heeh*, the devil has not made a very good fight of this.'

'Carefully, Simba,' I urged, 'Shaitan knows many tricks.'

Daudi was being very practical. 'Bwana,' he said, 'let us get the first payment of cows made, and then the whole betrothal is finished.'

'But,' said Simba, 'my cows are a day's safari away.'

'Then buy some others,' said Daudi. 'Bwana will lend you thirty shillings.'

'*Heeh*, but I have thirty-two shillings myself.'

'Well, Simba, in these days of the tax collection you can buy cows for ten shillings each.'

For a quarter of an hour they discussed cows – the humpbacked, sturdy little creatures that produce a maximum of a pint of milk a day, and serve as the native currency for Central Tanganyika.

When Daudi came back from the gate I tackled him: 'I think it's a bad thing for a man to buy his wife with cows. Surely this is a bad custom.'

'*E-e-e-h*,' replied my African dispenser, 'surely it is you who do not understand, Bwana. You don't buy a wife with cows, rather the dowry is a sign of good faith – or perhaps, Bwana, it should be. A

man cannot leave his wife and get his cows back, unless she has broken tribal laws. Also, if a man ill-treats his wife, behold, she may be taken back to her father's house by her people, and the cows may not be paid back.'

'But how can they fix these things, Daudi? Surely there must be many fights.'

'*Ng'o*, Bwana.' Daudi shook his head. 'The Chief hears the *sharui*, the case, and judges it.'

'Mmmm, Daudi, there is more in it than you see at one glance with European eyes.'

The dispenser laughed. 'Bwana, don't you think we ought to go and tell Perisi about this matter? After all, she's more in it than anyone except Simba.'

Together we set off towards the C.M.S. Girl's' School, and stopped under a tree to thank God for answering our prayers. For a while we were quiet, then I said, 'Daudi, it says in God's Book that if we abide in Jesus, that is, keep very close to Him, and walk in His way – and if His words abide in us – that is, if we obey what the Bible says – then we shall ask what we wish and it will happen.'

'That is true, Bwana, we have seen it today.'

'But, Daudi, God does not allow the path to be easy always, and I can well imagine the devil even now planning to upset things, Simba's faith particularly.'

'But why, Bwana? Why does God allow this?'

'*Kah*, Daudi, a man who hunts only rats never gets great courage, nor does he learn jungle craft. It's hunting lion and leopard that builds skill – avoiding tooth and claw – see?'

The African nodded. 'It's to make our souls fit and strong and usefully active.'

'That's it. Temptation is just like that; it's a challenge to make us use the special things available to those who become God's children.'

A schoolgirl came running up the path with a note in her hand. Panting, she stopped, I read it and handed it on to Daudi. Slowly he read it out loud:

'Perisi has suddenly collapsed. Please come at once. She looks deathly.'

11
The Danger List

The native bed with its criss-cross rope mattress seemed to shudder in sympathy with the shivering African girl who lay upon it. Her teeth chattered and the whole of her body shook uncontrollably. I felt her pulse. It had that rapid bouncy quality which meant fever. I scribbled a prescription and handed it to Daudi. He ran off to the dispensary to make up the draught. As I stood there waiting for the shivering fit to subside I knew that the girl was extremely ill. I turned to Sechelela, who had come down from the hospital.

'Sechie, have you heard whether Perisi has been away from school lately? Has she been visiting any of the villages or going anywhere on safari?'

'*Heeh*,' said the old African, 'Bwana, was it not a week ago that she went across beyond the swamp in the direction of the Ruaha river? Bwana, this is a land of stagnant water and many mosquitoes, and every variety of *dudu*.'

'*Ho*,' I said, 'well now, that's interesting. I suppose it all comes down to this, that she's got a very bad attack of malaria, and yet – somehow...' I shook my head in doubt.

Daudi arrived, breathless, with the medicine. We propped the girl up, and she swallowed it down with a gulp. Soon she was quieter. In a weak voice she said:

'Bwana, in the house where I stayed there was not only *mizuguni*, the mosquito, but *mikutupa*, the tick. *Kah*, many of them, Bwana. They came out at night and attacked me. Behold, I found fifteen on me in the morning – great big brutes, the size of the large joint of your thumb.'

The old African nurse nodded her head. '*Hee*... Bwana, that's more likely. Perhaps she has two diseases at once.'

Under Daudi's arm was a tin. He opened the lid and looked at me questioningly. I nodded. He produced a glass slide as big as a train ticket, a bottle of methylated spirit, and a bayonet-pointed needle. The African girl's thumb was rubbed for a moment briskly with cotton wool. Then a quick stab with the needle and a drop of blood was obtained. This was carefully placed on the slide. Daudi wiped the thumb with cotton wool and methylated spirit, and said:

'*Heeh*, Bwana, we'll know soon. The microscope will tell us the story of what is the trouble.'

'*Kah*, Daudi, I hope you're right, but somehow, I don't like it.'

'Bwana,' said the girl, 'in the place where there are giraffes and many trees and also many beautiful butterflies, behold, while I stopped to look at a trap set beside a water-hole to catch a leopard, behold, Bwana, I was attacked by many *mbungo.*'

'Tsetse flies,' said Daudi under his breath.

I whistled softly. 'Perhaps, Daudi, this is sleeping-sickness. I only hope your slide will show something.'

For half an hour we looked at that slide, looking at every possible corner, but there was not a sign of malaria or tick fever or of a peculiar-looking creature technically called a trypanosome, which produces sleeping-sickness. Daudi had once rather aptly described these deadly little brutes as looking like a sausage with a sail.

That evening Perisi was brought to hospital. She lay in bed with a temperature of 104, dangerously ill, suffering from a fever which I could not diagnose. I sat down with a piece of paper in front of me and worked out the possibilities. Most likely it was malaria. Often you could not find the tiny purple signet rings that indicate malaria inside the pink peach-petal-like red blood cells. So I decided to treat her as a malarial case. Very carefully I injected quinine into one of her veins.

It was dusk as I came away from the hospital. Crows were flying overhead; others, perching on the baobab tree, looked at me with their beady eyes and cawed. From somewhere behind me a stone whizzed and they went flapping and complaining to a baobab tree farther away. Behind me was Simba.

'Bwana,' he said, '*habari gani*? What news?'

'*Habari njema,* the news is good,' I replied, following the African formula, 'but she is very sick.'

'Bwana, what can I do?'

'There is nothing you can do in the ordinary way, Simba, but I want you to ask God to help me find out how to deal with Perisi's fever.'

'*Kah*, Bwana,' said the African. 'I will do that with strength and great pleading.'

I laid my hand on his shoulder.

'Don't forget, my friend, that it says in God's Book, "If two of you agree about anything you ask for, it will be done for you by my Father in heaven." Those words, Simba, were spoken by Jesus Himself. We are agreed in this. Let us both ask God.'

He nodded. '*Heeh*, Bwana, behold, it is more than a worthwhile thing to follow the ways of God.'

I watched his stalwart figure swinging through the greyness of early evening.

Out of the hospital gate came a strange-looking figure, wrapped in a magenta blanket.

'Bwana,' came a high-pitched voice, 'Bwana, oh Bwana, you must help me. Bwana, you must, you must. My daughter shall not die. She must not die, she shall not die. If she dies what will happen to my wealth? How can I obtain a dowry for a dead girl?'

I felt my hand clench. The voice became more wheedling. 'Bwana, give her the right medicine. You give her the right medicine and I'll pay you a cow – a cow, Bwana, to make my daughter better. Bwana, give her the best medicine, the strongest that you've got, that you use for yourself.'

Words just surged up within me but, fortunately, I didn't have to use them. Daudi got in first. He grasped the magenta blanket and pulled the African, wrapped in it, towards him.

'You go back to bed,' he said. 'Do not incur the great anger of the Bwana, who is not interested in money. He doesn't want your cows. He would have great joy to save the life of your daughter, but not for the reason of greed.'

'*Hongo*,' I said, turning on my heel, 'all he thinks about is not his daughter's health or her life, but the wretched cows he'll get for her dowry.'

Against the horizon I could see Simba silhouetted against the night sky. He was thinking only of helping the girl whom he loved in the way that he knew was most effective. Closer to me was the shuffling figure of Perisi's father – his fat unlovely figure somehow in keeping with his greediness of mind.

A week went by – a week during which the African girl slowly grew worse. Without a clear-cut diagnosis I had employed what we called shotgun therapy, trying this or that drug or treatment, and hoping that one of them would strike the cause. But none of the medicines did much good, and Perisi slowly went downhill.

12
Struggle on the Brink

I looked up from the carefully traced temperature chart.

'You know, Sister, I don't think there's any doubt about it now. Perisi has typhoid. It was just as well we put her where we did and treated her as infectious, or we might have had an epidemic on our hands.'

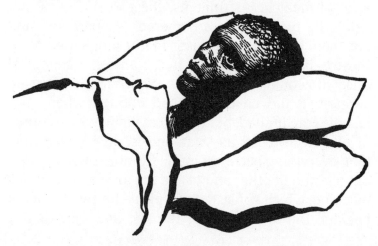

I looked down at the African girl. She was dreadfully ill. Her eyes seemed to have sunk in while her cheek bones stuck out sharply. Her lips were dry and parched. I turned to the white nurse who stood beside me.

'You know, Sister, I'm afraid you must keep completely away from this girl. If you're going to look after all the mothers and babies in the place we can't afford to let you come near this infectious spot. I'll get old Sechelela to sit here and do this special job. She'll look after Perisi day and night, in a way that nobody else could.'

So it was that I sat on the steps with Sechelela and outlined the things that she was to look for.

'*Hulicize*,' I said, 'listen – these are the things that you must look for. If she shivers, or complains of sudden sharp pains in her stomach, or if her pulse rate becomes faster, let me know at once, whether it be day or night. Behold, this is the time of great danger.'

Before leaving the hospital that afternoon I collected a lot of medical instruments, the sort of things that would be required for an emergency operation, and put them inside the steriliser in our jungle operating theatre, hoping as I did so that if any emergency did arise, it wouldn't happen at night. To do intricate surgery in the daytime is bad enough when your facilities are limited, but to do it at night, with a couple of electric torches as your only source of lighting, then everything becomes infinitely more difficult. I got out a bottle of ether and tested my jungle anaesthetic machine, which consisted of a pickle bottle, a football bladder, the foot-pump of the car, and four or five

122

yards of fine rubber tubing. Everything was ready for an emergency at a minute's notice. As I went to open the door I heard a deep voice:

'*Hodi*, Bwana.'

I recognised Simba's voice.

'*Karibu*, Come in,' I replied.

'Bwana,' said the African, 'do you believe that God is stronger than Shaitani?'

'I do, Simba, why?'

'Bwana, I have heard many words these days. It is said in the village that the Chief, Makaranga, has caused spells to be cast, not only against Mafuta, but also against Perisi. Bwana, this is the work of spells. Spells are very powerful, Bwana. People die in our country of Ugogo often, nearly always, when one as strong as this is made. I have fear, Bwana.'

'*Kah*, Simba, you have seen the strength of God in the matter of the betrothal – was not that enough?'

The tall African shivered slightly. He gripped my shoulder and shook his head doubtfully.

'*Hongo*, Simba, have no fear. The devil is powerless when God is fighting on behalf of those of His family.'

Simba's eyes were wide open. He rolled them and said, '*Hongo!*'

I tapped him gently on the chest with my forefinger. 'Listen and I will tell you a story of what happened in the days of long ago when Eleya – the preacher – was working and when Ahabu was the king.' Simba sat down, his chin in his hands, his eyes held mine as I continued. 'Behold, in those days there were many witch-doctors who spent all their time worshipping and offering sacrifices to their *mulungu,* their god, whom they called Baal. Many people in those days also said that Baal was stronger than Almighty God, so Eleya was by himself. He challenged those who followed the false god and said to them: "Let us each take an ox, and prepare it for an offering – and then let us each call upon our god and ask him to bring fire to burn up the offering. Then whichever god answers, let him be the god for everyone to follow." And all the people said, "*Heeh*, that is a fair thing, that is wise." And so Eleya told his five hundred rivals to select their ox. This they did. They killed and put it upon the altar. Behold, they started to dance, to sing and to shout. *Kumbe!* As they danced they became more and more frenzied. They cut themselves with stones, they screamed. The people stood by and watched, enthralled. They expected the fire to come. But no fire came. Eleya stood there with a little smile on his face.

'"Go on," he shouted, "make much noise; perhaps your god is asleep, or perhaps he's on a journey."

'They yelled and chanted and made an even greater noise, and said, "O Baal, O Baal, hear" – but there was no voice, nor any answer. They leaped upon the altar frothing at the mouth. Behold, when the sun was high in the heavens Eleya mocked them again and said "Go on, cry louder, for he is a god. Perhaps he's talking, or perhaps he's chasing someone. Perhaps he's on safari. Cry loudly, wake him up – he must be asleep."

'And behold their frenzy grew, but no fire appeared. Time passed, their dance went on until the sun was well on its way, and then Eleya said, in a tone that everyone obeyed, "Come near." And all the people came close to him. Then he built up the altar of God. He built it with great stones, twelve of them. Then he dug a deep trench around the altar. On the stones he put wood, on the wood the cut-up bits of bullock, and then he called for four great pots of water, which were poured over the top of the meat and the wood and the stones and ran down and filled the trenches.'

'*Kah*, Bwana,' said Simba, 'but the water would stop the wood from burning. That was unwise.'

'*Haah*, that's what Eleya thought. He wanted to show the people that there were no tricks in what he was doing; that it was God Almighty who worked; that God was very much more powerful than the people could ever think. Then everything was ready. All was quiet, even the *waganga,* the witchdoctors, were quiet. Eleya lifted up his hands to heaven, and said, "O God, let it be known this day that you are God, that I am your servant, and that I have done all these things at your command. Hear me, O God, hear me, that the people may know that you are the God of gods." And as he prayed the fire of God fell and burnt up the sacrifice and the wood and even the stones, and the dust from the trench that they had dug, and the water that was in it.

All the people were amazed. They were terrified, and they cried, "He is the God. God, He is the God of gods."'

Slowly Simba nodded his head. 'Bwana, is that story true?'

'Yes, Simba, that is true all right. You can read it for yourself in the Bible, in the Book of Kings. What's more, the God who lived in those days is the God whom we serve and whom we worship, and He is the God who is going to help us win in this tremendous fight against evil, and against the wrong way.'

For a quarter of an hour we knelt together, and told God all about the situation once again, and asked Him, as He had shown His power in the days of Eleya, the prophet, that He would do the same in Tanganyika, in the saving of the life of the African girl who was His follower.

It was almost dark in the theatre when we got up from our knees. I opened the door and saw hurrying towards me a figure carrying a hurricane lantern. Sechelela's voice came out of the darkness, 'Bwana, quickly, come and see Perisi at once. She has started to shiver. She says there is a very sudden bad pain here.' She put her hand over the area where the appendix normally resides. 'Bwana, I have never seen her look so ill, never.'

I hurried back with her to the ward and made a careful examination, and as point by point was made my heart sank lower and lower. There was only one thing to be done, and that was an immediate and urgent operation. In typhoid there was always the deadly danger of perforation of the bowel. I knew that with things as they were in our jungle hospital, she had perhaps one in ten chance of recovery, humanly speaking. And then I seemed to feel as Elijah, the prophet, must have felt. Calm confidence seemed to come upon me. Quietly I made the arrangements for her to be brought to the theatre. Standing outside was Simba. He said:

'What's happened?'

'Simba,' I said, 'it's as though the water had been thrown over everything as in the story that I told you. This seems the darkest hour. Perisi's life is at the very door of the village of death, and yet, black as everything appears, somehow I feel –'

Simba interrupted. 'Bwana, so do I. Behold, is it not what the Bible calls, "the peace of God which passes all understanding"?'

I opened the door of the operating theatre. Simba barred my way:

'Bwana, I must help in this operation.'

'There's nothing you can do my friend, nothing.'

'Bwana,' said Sechelela, 'there is one thing he could do. If we put a mask round his mouth, and a cap on his head and a gown on his body he could stand on a box and hold your big electric torch. He would hold it with strength so that it would not waver right throughout the operation.'

'Bwana,' said the African, 'let me do that.'

'*Viswanu*,' I said, 'you shall do that, but there must not be one flicker of that torch through the work, and it may take two hours.'

The primus was roaring away underneath the steriliser in the theatre. Daudi was skilfully putting out the various instruments and dressings that would be required for the operation. Two African lads carried the dangerously-ill girl into the theatre and very gently laid her on the table. I prepared for the anaesthetic.

Her lips moved. I put my ear near. 'Bwana,' she said, 'perhaps I will die?'

'Perhaps,' I whispered in reply, 'but do not forget, Perisi, that as I work tonight, the hand of the Master is on my hand.'

'Bwana,' she said, looking up at me with a smile, 'and I can feel His hand with me holding.' And then she said, 'Bwana, what of Simba?'

I heard a sharply-taken breath behind me. 'Perisi,' I said, 'he is here. It is he that will hold the light for this work.'

I put out my hand and drew the strong African down beside me. 'Bwana,' she said, 'tell him that my heart still calls and calls.' And then she recognised the face looking over my shoulder. Although she could only see his eyes, there was something in those eyes which I have rarely seen in the eyes of anyone, black or white.

'Come,' I said, picking up the anaesthetic mask, 'and as you sleep, Perisi, and as we work, let us have the one word from God in our hearts – here it is: "Let not your heart be troubled, neither let it be afraid."'

I think everyone in that jungle operating theatre prayed intensely as the minutes ticked by on the dilapidated alarm clock which stood on the window-sill.

The operation was extremely intricate, but at last it was done. From start to finish I had been able to see splendidly. There was not a flicker in the beam of that powerful electric torch held directly over my left shoulder. As I put in the last few stitches, the batteries obviously were failing.

'Bwana,' said the deep voice behind me, 'do not wait for those who will come with a stretcher. Behold, I can carry her in my arms to the ward, as you would a sick child.'

I walked beside him as he carried the girl he loved back to the ward. I could hear the words he kept whispering over and over again. *Gwe go Mulungo u mulungu lungu,* Oh Almighty God, Almighty God.

With infinite gentleness he put the girl down on the bed and stood back while Sechelela made her comfortable.

'Wait outside, Simba,' I said, 'I'll be with you before long.'

I gave the girl an injection and waited. It was a matter of two hours before she was safely out of the anaesthetic, and then I came out into the cold, clear moonlight of the Tanganyikan night. Simba was pacing up and down.

'Bwana,' he said, 'when will we know whether she will recover?'

'That's hard to say, Simba, but within a week we should know. And if she sleeps tonight it will make all the difference.'

'In a week, Bwana.' He shook his head. 'But what shall I do during that week?'

'We'll need food to strengthen her. More than just the porridge of the hospital. She will need strong soup. Soup that must be made from meat. Can you...?'

Simba laughed aloud in his relief.

'*Kah*, Bwana, can I get meat? Why, I'll go hunting! Perisi will have the food that she requires.'

'Good man,' I replied, 'and now, you go to bed and get some sleep so that your hunting may be successful at dawn.'

It was two in the morning when an African nurse came to report to me that at last Perisi had fallen into a deep sleep.

'*Viswanu*, that's good,' I replied, 'now try and keep the place as quiet as you possibly can. Every bit of sleep that she can get is all to the good. Sleep above everything will help if only...'

At that moment came a piercing shriek; the eerie melancholy howl that an African lets out when someone has died. I bolted for the hospital. It came again and again, high pitched and horrible. At all costs that noise had to be stopped. Daudi and Kefa apparently had the same idea, for when I arrived at the hospital they were forcibly holding down Mafuta.

Daudi had the fat man's face covered with one of the towels from the out-patient's room.

'Bwana,' he panted, 'I tried to stop him by putting my hand over his mouth, but he bit me, so I quietened him with a towel.'

A grunt came from the figure on the ground.

I bent down and said, 'Take the towel away for a minute, Daudi,' – and to Mafuta, 'Don't you dare to raise your voice.'

In a whining tone he said, 'But Bwana, she's going to die. And if she dies, behold, I will be a poor man. And, Bwana, if I'm poor, what will I do, what will I do?'

He got no further, for the towel went back into place, and his wail ended in a gurgle. I went into the dispensary, lifted my hurricane lantern till I could find the appropriate bottle, and poured him a large dose of bromide mixture. I personally supervised his drinking of this, and then I saw that he was put back to bed. I turned to Kefa:

'Stay with him until he sleeps. Do not leave him under any circumstances. Now I will go and see what damage he has done to his daughter by his wailing.'

In the ward Sechelela was looking after Perisi. The old African nurse seemed to sense that someone was coming. She put her head out of the door, and seeing me, put her fingers to her lips.

'Bwana,' she said, 'that noise disturbed her. She's lying there half asleep, half awake. But I think she'll go to sleep again. She's muttering, "What shall I do?"

I went quietly across the concrete floor to the bed and stooped over her.

Perisi was conscious, and in English she said to me, 'Bwana, my mouth is as dry as the sole of a sandal.' She ran her dry tongue round her cracked lips.

I lifted a cup of water to her lips. She sipped.

'*Heeh*,' she said, sinking back on the pillows. 'Bwana, that's good. Bwana, I don't think I'll be able to sleep. Behold, I have great pain.'

'Perisi, you have pain, but sleep you will, because…' With that I carefully injected morphia.

'*Heeh*,' said the girl, 'Bwana, will that bring relief?'

I nodded in the half darkness. She let out a little sigh and seemed to be asleep. I stood there in the complete silence of the African night. Suddenly I was aware of a figure outside the door frantically beckoning me. It was Daudi. I tiptoed across to him.

'Bwana,' he whispered hoarsely, 'quickly, run, run for your life.'

13
Death and Decision

'Bwana,' said Daudi, as we ran, 'it's Mafuta. Something dreadful has happened to him. He's collapsed. He looks awful.'

We raced through the gate into the men's ward garden and I was struck by the clear-cut shadow of the pomegranate tree that grew beside the gate, on the white wall of the ward. It's strange how these impressions seem to burn their way into your memory. In the ward I found an anxious-looking African dispenser propping up the fat man. My fingers were on his pulse. Some sixth sense within me seemed to vibrate. Death seemed to be already in the man.

Hastily we lighted a little spirit lamp and prepared an injection. Soon Mafuta was lying back on his pillow while morphia did its merciful work.

'Bwana,' said Daudi anxiously in a whisper, 'we did not hurt him, did we, when we struggled with him out there when he made all that noise?'

'No, Daudi, this is the result of a lot of things. The life that Mafuta has lived has been a hectic one.'

The African raised his right eyebrow: '*Hongo*, Bwana, truly!'

'You know, Daudi, it says in the Bible that if we sow the wind we'll reap the whirlwind, and in another place it says, 'Make no mistake, you can't laugh at God. Whatever a man sows, he'll reap.' Mafuta now is getting the harvest of all the things he has done, and what a crop!'

For two hours the African lay there quite unconscious. Suddenly he sighed, my fingers on his wrist felt the pulse flicker and stop. From outside the window came the blood-freezing yell of death, followed by almost solid silence.

'*Kah*, Bwana,' whispered Daudi, 'that was one of the spies of the Chief Makaranga.'

The dawning was not far off when Daudi and I left the ward.

We stood looking out over the plains and listening to the throb of drums in a village near at hand.

My companion touched my arm.

'Bwana, the news is being carried. Behold, it will soon be known over the countryside that Mafuta has gone to his ancestors. That will mean trouble. Behold, I heard today that Mafuta had accepted three cows from Makaranga, but already he had sold them. Behold, the Chief will now demand his cows back, and it will be the responsibility of Mafuta's relations to pay them back, unless the Chief still wants to marry Perisi.'

Daudi shook his head. He was very puzzled. 'I have heard, Bwana, that the only relation that Mafuta has here, has gone away because he was a man of small courage. He feared that the trouble that always followed the fat man would come his way. And so, Bwana, *heh*, the Chief can claim Perisi, unless…'

'*Kah*,' said Daudi, 'if there were no relations then the foster parents, the people who looked after the girl, they would have the right to claim the dowry. Is she not one of their family?'

'Right,' I said, 'who looked after Perisi?'

'*Heh*,' said Daudi, 'was she not looked after at the C.M.S. school?'

A dark shadow was thrown on the wall – an African coming towards us with a large spear. The shadow made him look absolutely immense.

'*Kah*,' whispered Daudi, 'who is this?'

A minute later a voice came. '*Hodi, Hodi*? May I come in?'

Daudi hurried to the gate and opened it. There stood Simba. '*Kah*,' he said, 'I have heard the news through the voices of the drums. I have come to help.'

'Simba,' I said, 'we're in big trouble. Behold, there are no relations to look after Mafuta's burial. There are no relations to pay back to the Chief the cows that had been received from him.'

'*Kah*,' said Simba, 'not only that, Bwana, but tomorrow, early tomorrow, you will find people coming here from Makaranga – demanding to talk to Perisi, and she will be upset, and perhaps, perhaps, Bwana, it may be too much for her.'

'I can deal with that if —'

'Simba eagerly interrupted. 'Bwana, I can deal with many things. Behold, I can pay the cows back. Behold, Bwana, I will do the work of relative. Anything, anything at all, I will do.'

'Then between us it looks as though we can cope with this difficulty.'

Simba nodded.

And there in the first light, quietly standing there, we bowed our heads, and asked God to help us to straighten out this tangle, and help us to travel the right path through it all. For a while all was quiet, then Simba traced figures on the dust of the floor with his great toe.

'Bwana,' he said, 'I have been thinking. Behold, when the sun set Mafuta had the power to choose which way his life would go, but behold, now, he has no chance to choose. The door of death has slammed suddenly.'

'*Heeh*,' said Daudi, 'and was it not only in the late afternoon that I spoke to him just in this place. I told him that the way of riches was a very slippery way. I reminded him of the story that Jesus told about the man whose crops were great. The man who said within his heart that he had much riches and much food for many years, but God said to him, "Foolish man, this night shall your soul be demanded from you. Then whose will your possessions be?"

'Bwana,' said Daudi, 'I told him all this, but he would not listen, and I told him that the biggest sin of all, bigger than the sin of murder, and the breaking of any or all of the commandments, was turning your back on God and showing no interest in the gift of life which Jesus offers, and bought at such very, very great cost. But Bwana, he would not listen. He just said "*Kah*, I have no interest." Bwana, that was only a matter of hours ago, and now, where is his soul?'

'Perhaps, Daudi,' said Simba, 'this will serve as a strong warning to other people who hear about it.'

With this sombre thought I left them, and walked across the cornfields to my house.

I was about to have breakfast when, looking through the window, I saw an imposing procession winding its way up the hill towards the hospital. In the middle of a group of Africans, dressed in all sorts of clothes, was a Chief, a red fez on his head. He was wearing a check tweed coat over the long flowing white nightshirt-like *kanzu* that Africans love to wear.

'Bwana,' said Daudi, who had hurried towards my place, 'here comes Makaranga; he is a man of great trouble.'

'See that the hospital gate is shut and locked, Daudi, and ask the Chief if he would be good enough to come to the house of discussion, that we may drink tea and talk over these things, but see that Perisi is kept from any noise.'

So it was that some quarter of an hour later I shook hands ceremoniously with the Chief and his retinue. Daudi and Simba sat beside me on three-legged stools. We talked about many things in African fashion before we actually got down to the matter at stake.

Suddenly Simba started to his feet. He hurried to the door and said in a loud voice, 'Behold, Mazengo, the great Chief of Ugogo has arrived.'

Everybody stood up as the fine old African leader came into the room. Smiling all over his face he shook hands all round and sat down.

Nobody in the whole country could help in the way he could. His judgment was utterly unbiased, and his word law.

'*Mutemi*, Chief,' I said, 'it is good to see you here. Behold, we have a big word to discuss and your wisdom will be of great help. Is not this so?' I turned to Makaranga.

'*Heeh*, Bwana, it is so.'

So I told him the story which, apparently, he knew all about.

'Bwana,' said the king, 'it is our custom that the cows must be paid back by the relations of the man who has died unless the one who has paid them still wants to marry.'

He turned to Makaranga with his eyebrows raised in question.

'*Koh*,' said the Chief, playing with the ornate buttons of his coat, 'and if I did not want to marry her, why should I have paid over the cows?'

'*Hongo*,' said the old African king quietly, 'but the Bwana tells me that this moment the girl is very ill and even now she is walking close to the gates of death.'

'*Kah*,' said Makaranga, 'behold these are the words of the Bwana. He does not desire the girl to marry me. Is there not another whom he favours?'

I looked across at Simba whose face was absolutely expressionless. I felt that things were going remarkably badly. Suddenly Sechelela's face appeared round the door.

'Bwana,' she called, with urgency in her voice, 'Bwana, are you there?'

'Yes,' I said, stepping forward.

'Bwana, Perisi has ceased to breathe. She...'

I waited for no more but ran, followed by Daudi and Simba. Crouching beside the girl's bedside, with my stethoscope to my ears, I listened to her heart. There was the faintest of beats. I turned towards the door. Simba was standing with an agonised question in his eyes. Before speaking a word I picked up the syringe, ready for just such an emergency as this, and injected rapidly. Then I went across to the African.

'Simba, there was a time when you lay as she lies now, very close to death. Your need then is her need now. In the days of your need she gave you blood.'

'*Hongo*,' said Simba, a smile coming over his face, 'that's something I can do. Bwana, I'll give her a *debe* full.'

Now a *debe* is a four-gallon kerosene tin.

I hurried across to the pathology room to make the necessary test and do the transfusion at top speed.

Even as I hurried I saw an African who was a stranger to me running through the hospital gate. I heard the story later how he panted into the room where the fateful discussion about Perisi's life was going on, and whispered into Makaranga's ear, 'The girl is even now dying; get your cows quickly, before you lose them.'

All in a minute the situation was changed.

'*Kah*,' said Makaranga, 'I will have back my cows. There is no profit in a wife who has no strength. Let the matter be settled now.'

'Well,' said the king, 'the cows will be paid over to you at sunset tonight, as is our custom. The *shauri* is finished.'

It was an hour before sunset when the last few ounces of blood ran safely into Perisi's veins. Simba sat on the floor, watching my every movement. I removed the needle and put a little square of sticking-plaster over the place where it had been.

I listened again with my stethoscope. This time the heart sounds came through cheerfully and strongly.

'All is well, Simba. Now run off and collect those cows for the Chief.' I stood up and stretched. 'Behold, what a day it's been, but surely, all things work together for good to those who love God.'

He nodded. 'I can't quite remember the words at the end, Bwana, but they go like this, "To those people whom He has called, to those who obey Him and do His work."'

'It's true,' I said. 'Well, off you go, lion man. Come back to see me tomorrow here at a little after dawn and I'll tell you everything.'

In the grey light of the early morning I walked up to the ward. Sechelela had been up all night. She met me at the steps.

'Bwana, Perisi has slept for twelve hours and has wakened this morning, only a few minutes ago, better than I have seen her for weeks.'

14

Convalescence

Three weeks later I stood on the veranda and looked beyond the operating theatre. Out of the thornbush and into the glare of the plains came two figures – a tall man, and the second a small person. I couldn't make out whether it was a boy or a girl. Each of them seemed to be carrying a load on their back. When they were still half a mile away, I could hear the cheery

voice of the man in front, chanting an African hunting song. As they came closer I could hear the shrill treble of the girl who walked behind, joining in the chorus to the song that was being sung.

'*Heh*,' said Daudi, 'that, Bwana, must be Simba, and Simba has great joy.'

'Behold, perhaps he is bringing us something which will bring strength to our hearts, Daudi.'

'*Heh*, Bwana, and to our stomachs also.'

At that moment round the corner of the hospital building came Simba, over his shoulders a buck that he had shot with his bow and arrow. Behind him, a small girl, whose face was familiar. On her shoulders was no burden of venison, but a huge lump, rather bigger than her head. I recognised her as the child from Makali who had disappeared when there were rumours of witchcraft. But when her relatives heard the news that Perisi, whom they had regarded as being good as dead, was very much alive, and that Simba was going to the hospital with meat on his shoulder, they agreed that the small girl should accompany him. At first her father had been a bit reticent because he felt that he might be asked to pay a fee for the operation and medicines. This, of course, was the usual thing with the witch-doctor. But Simba laughed, and said that the load that he carried on his shoulder would be so used that the load on the small girl's shoulder might be removed for ever.

He lowered the buck down at my feet.

'Bwana,' he said, 'I have walked many miles from right over there.' He raised the pitch of his voice and pointed with his chin towards a group of baobab trees, five or six miles away. '*Heeh*, behold, will I not sit in the shade and watch others prepare the meal, and then we will have stew.'

Daudi and Samson carried the animal behind the native kitchen and on a sheet of old iron started doing some primitive butchery. Simba was standing as though he had no interest in things, but I could see his eyes roving round the place. Suddenly on the veranda of the women's ward, walking slowly, and with some difficulty, I saw Perisi.

'*Heh*,' said Simba, dropping his voice so that only I would hear, 'she walks, Bwana. *Kah!* But look at her. Ooh, she's thin. *Heeh*, surely she needs all that meat that I can obtain for her.'

'Come over,' I said, 'and we will greet her.'

We walked across, and in the usual African fashion, said, '*Mbwuka*, good day.'

She replied, '*Mbukwa*.' The greetings went on for quite a while as African greetings do, and then I said:

'But how do you feel these days, Perisi?'

'Bwana,' she said, 'how should you feel when you had been sewed up like an old shirt? *Kumbe!* My skin bites when I stretch it.'

I laughed. She sat down on the three-legged stool, and leant against the cool stonework of the wall. Simba crouched down on his haunches, holding his spear, and suddenly I found it necessary to go about thirty or forty yards away and look out over the plain. The burning heat of the afternoon sun seemed to billow in waves over the dry earth. There were a collection of crows sitting restlessly on the bare limbs of a baobab tree. I smiled to myself and wondered what Simba was saying to Perisi.

Then I heard a voice behind me. 'Bwana.' I looked round: it was the small girl who had come with Simba. 'Bwana,' she said, 'when will you bring help to me?'

I looked at her shoulder, covered with a dry black African cloth. Gently I removed it and felt the great unsightly knob that was on her back. It was as large as her head. To my satisfaction it was not attached to her spine or to any vital structure. I walked with her across to the ward. Sechelela came out.

'Sechie,' I said, 'see that this child has several baths.' The old African woman wrinkled up her nose and smiled at me.

'*Heh*, Bwana, it shall be done,' she chuckled.

'And while you're doing it, I will see how soon I can find opportunity in our operating theatre to remove the burden from her shoulders.'

I went and checked up on the instruments that would be required for what did not look like a very difficult operation, but was one which would certainly bring tremendous relief to the small girl. Simba had told me that she was the laughter of her companions because of her *cigongo,* the burden, on her back.

There was the smell of stew coming from a great pot. A group of nurses and hospital folk were standing round keenly interested.

Perisi from her chair was telling them a story.

'Behold,' she said, 'it happened this way. Once there was a man called Mukristo, and in the story that I read behold he had great sadness, and wept very much,

and cried with a voice full of sadness, "What shall I do, what shall I do?"

'His wife said to him, "Why have you grief?"

'He said, "Am I not in great trouble by reason of the burden that lies hard upon me?"' The little girl shivered, but Perisi put out her arm and drew her to her.

She continued, 'Behold, he was walking one day reading in his book, and as he read the sadness welled up within him and he cried out with a loud voice, "What shall I do, what shall I do to be saved from this burden?"

'And even as he cried, one came to him: "*Heh*,"' said this one, "why have you grief?"

'"Behold," said Mukristo, "I have read in this book that the name of the burden on my back is sin, and I fear that this burden will sink me lower than the grave."

'"*Kah*," said his companion, "if that is your condition why do you stand here still?"

'"*Hongo*, where will I go?" asked Mukristo.

'He was pointed along the way that led through swamps, through the jungle where lions were, past places where there were enemies, mountains with vast smoke, through the country where the giants are, until he came to a place where on a hill there stood a wooden cross. Seeing the cross, Mukristo stood still and looked, and as he looked, he wondered, and then he suddenly moved forward and went up the hill to the place where the cross stood. And as he stood there, suddenly his burden loosened itself from his shoulders and began to tumble, and roll down the hill, and was gone for ever. *Hongo!* Then was Mukristo glad and full of joy and he said with a merry heart, "He has given me rest by His sorrow, and life by His death."'

The small girl touched Perisi on the arm. 'Why did the burden fall off when he looked at the cross of wood?'

Perisi told her of the Son of God who had been nailed on that cross to take away the punishment for our sins, and how He had died.

Tears ran down the little girl's face. '*Kah*,' she said, 'but you must love Him.'

Simba and Perisi nodded their heads. 'We do. We have great reason to love Him,' they said. It seemed the words came out together. 'You, too, will understand these things,' said Perisi, gently. 'Behold, the Bwana will help you and the burden will go from your back, and then you will understand when you have lost your *cigongo*, which gives you shame and sorrow, you will understand perhaps better than anybody, how sin brings shame, sorrow, pain, sadness.'

The little girl nodded her head. The next day at that same hour we carried her into the operating theatre, and at sundown as she came out of the anaesthetic she looked up into the smiling eyes of Perisi and the first words that came to her lips were, 'It's gone, my *cigongo* has gone.'

'*Heh*,' said the African girl, 'truly, it's gone! There are many stories of Jesus that I will tell you these days as you and I get strong.'

'Perisi,' I said, as she came to the door, 'you must lie down. You've been doing many things these days. You have much strength to gain.'

'Bwana,' said the African girl, 'I have great joy in my heart. These days I have learnt many things. Behold, do I not hear with great joy how Simba tells the words of God as he goes from village to village? He has joy in his heart and laughter in his mouth, and Bwana,' she dropped her voice, 'behold, when he and I work together, those will be days of great joy.'

15
The Cows

Simba was sitting on a petrol box while Daudi trimmed his hair with a pair of scissors, then deftly cut a parting through the tight curls with a rusty razor blade.

'There,' said my African dispenser, '*heh*, behold, you look very much as one should look, and when you come out in your new shorts and your shirt, behold, there will not be another in the country to compare with you.'

Simba smiled. There were deep cuts over his cheek bones where, as a small child, his parents had set to work to beautify his face. There was scarring round his eyes, telling of our attempt to deal with a rather nasty eye condition, which was all too common in Tanganyika.

'*Heh*, Bwana,' said he, 'today I want your help. Behold, I would go down to speak to the *Wabibi*, the European teachers at the C.M.S. school, and ask them if they are willing that I should marry Perisi.'

I had discussed this matter with the teachers, not once, but a score of times, and the whole thing was as good as arranged, but according to African customs Simba had to go down and have a *shauri,* a discussion, regarding the dowry and all the various things that he should do.

'Bwana,' said he, 'it is our custom to take a companion to discuss these matters with the relations of the girl. Behold has not the Chief said that the *Wabibi* are the ones to whom I should go, and with whom I should discuss the dowry. Tell them, Bwana, that her father has asked me for twenty-eight cows. Bwana, see if you can get them to agree to twenty-five. Behold, there will be great joy then, and we will have some cows for a feast.'

'What,' I said, 'but didn't you pay three to the Chief Makaranga? Did not…'

'*Heh*, Bwana, but will they understand about that?'

'I'll tell them' I said, 'and we'll see what we can do.'

We stood outside the school. '*Bibi*,' I called, '*Hodi!* May I come in?'

'*Karibu*,' called the headmistress.

We went in. Simba looked rather self-conscious. He was brought a three-legged stool, and sat down while I carried on the discussion. I spoke in the native language.

'Behold,' I said, 'my friend has come asking for the hand of a child of the schoo, Perisi. He would have her for his wife.'

'*Heeh*,' said the headmistress, her eyes twinkling, 'but is he the right sort of person, whom I would wish to marry one of my children?'

'*Kah*,' I said, 'behold, these are difficult words. I'm afraid he is a man who is very fierce – a dangerous hunter – a man who perhaps would beat his wife.'

'*Yah*, Bwana,' said Simba. 'Behold...' and then he saw the twinkle in my eye and laughed. '*Heh*,' he said, and settled back on his stool.

'Simba suggested,' said I, 'that he should pay a dowry of twenty cows.' Simba's ears twitched.

'*O-o-o-h*,' said the headmistress in her best African fashion, 'behold, thirty cows...'

'*Yah*,' said I, following out what Daudi had taught me, 'behold, is he not a poor man, will you not accept twenty-four cows?'

'*Heeh*,' said the headmistress, '*yeeh*, perhaps we could agree to twenty-six?'

'*Kah*,' said I, 'behold he is a man of great sickness, behold, was he not attacked by a lion, and has he not been very helpful in the great sickness of Perisi? Perhaps without him she would not have lived.'

'*Heeh*,' said the headmistress, smiling, 'then perhaps twenty-five cows.'

Simba nodded his head to indicate to me to close with that bargain. Suddenly speaking in English, I said:

'Where are you going to put twenty-five cows?'

Laughingly the headmistress said, 'I've been wondering that too. Have you any suggestions?'

153

I turned to Simba: 'Simba, my friend, I want you to bring the cattle. They must all be *zingombe zinhukulu,* cows, for we plan to teach the children of the hospital how cows should be looked after, how they should be milked, so that the children may be given strength, so that the babies may be properly fed, and so that the ways of health may be brought before the women of the country.'

'*Heh,*' said Simba, 'those are words of wisdom. But, Bwana, it is our custom always to give many bulls in a dowry. Behold, there is more profit in a cow than a bull. Will not the Bibi agree to, say, twenty cows?'

And then an agreement was made that he should bring, not twenty, but twelve cows, and instead of the others that he should undertake to build a *boma*, a thornbush fence, in which the cattle would be kept to keep them safe from leopards and hyenas; and that he would set to work and collect grass and grow maize, that when the rainy season came, the cattle might be fed. All this would happen while Perisi was getting her strength back, and then in due course, would come the wedding.

As we walked back to the hospital, Simba tapped my arm:

'Bwana,' he said, 'behold, in truth, this is the place of joy. First I travelled this road, carried. My relations thought I was dying. But in the hospital I found life. *Heh*, Bwana, and I heard the words of God, and I found the bigger life that lasts when the body has gone, and then Bwana, to my life has come love. Behold, Bwana, everything is now arranged. Difficulties seemed to be everywhere. It seemed impossible that Perisi should ever be mine. But now, Bwana, *heh*, I walk this path, I live, I have strength, my heart sings, and behold, when I build my *kaya,* my house, I will build it and have a companion whose heart turns in the same direction as mine.'

We walked on in silence for a while. Then Simba stopped beside an oleander bush: '*Kah*, Bwana, you have come from your country to tell my people the words of God, and to help them; shall not I, a Mugugo tribesman, tell my own people the words of God? Shall not Perisi and I in our home show them the better way? She shall learn the words of health, and of the way of helping babies. Behold, I will learn more and more of reading, so that in our village we may be the ones to act as the signpost to point our own people to God. Bwana, as that signpost' – he pointed with his chin to the Mvumi Hospital – 'as that signpost, Bwana, shows the road to the road of healing, so Perisi and I in our house will point the way to Jesus, the Son of God. *Kah*, Bwana, at night we will sit round the fire and tell the people the stories of God. Have you heard Perisi? Has she not got a tongue? Does it not move sweetly and smoothly as she tells the story?'

We came to the hospital and went in through the gates. It was nearly dark, and on the veranda sat the dispensers and nurses. Amongst them I could see Perisi. She was a very different girl from the one who had hobbled round a fortnight before. She was strong, and well on the high road to health. I pointed her out to Simba.

'Behold,' I said, 'she is gaining strength.' At that moment they started to sing. Daudi and Kefa lifted their voices in a peculiar African tune of a hymn which went to familiar words.

Simba listened to them, and as they finished, he said, '*Kah*, Bwana, it is a very good thing to sing your thankfulness to God. Bwana, my voice is no good for singing as theirs is, but behold, I will live my thankfulness to Him.'

'That's the best way of doing it,' I replied. 'God does not often ask people to be ready to die for Him, although sometimes that's necessary; but He does ask them to live for Him. Behold, that is where you and Perisi can do big things.'

I put my hand on his shoulder as we came up to the group sitting on the veranda.

'Behold, the matter of the dowry is finished.'

Perisi and some of the nurses slipped inside the ward. This was their custom.

'Behold, it is my hope that before long the cows will be paid over, the dowry will be finished, and we will hear the drums of the village beating with joy for the wedding of Simba and Perisi.'

16
Marriage

There was a little mud-roofed African building at our hospital where folk did their ironing. A great umbrella-like palm tree spread its branches ten feet up over the entrance, shading those who worked inside. I was in our laboratory looking at blood slides, checking on people with malaria, when I saw Simba walking down the path towards the ironing-room. Under his arm were sundry garments, and he was dressed entirely in a yard-wide strip of ancient blanket, which was tied round his middle. He was carrying a gourd of hot coals. These he put into one of the charcoal irons that are used in Tanganyika. He waved it round in the air until it was hot and the coals glowed inside, and then began to iron the clothes he had brought with him.

First he set to work on a pale pink shirt. He seemed to be in considerable trouble when it came to the collar. He put this carefully aside, and then started on a pair of pale pink shorts.

I put the microscope away in its box, looked through the window and said, '*Hah*, Simba, why have you chosen that colour?'

The African hunter laughed. 'Bwana, when the grass is green, behold, the trees are green. In the days of dryness, the earth is brown, and so also is the grass. Behold, have I not given Perisi clothes of the pale red colour? Should I not wear the pale red colour also?'

He was very serious, so I had to restrain my mirth a little. He carefully blew the ashes out of the iron, placed it in the right position, and put the ironed clothing over his arm.

'Bwana,' came a breathless voice at the door. 'Quickly, come over to the children's ward, there is a baby with convulsions!'

I grabbed my *topee* and ran. As I ran, I saw Perisi.

'Perisi,' I said, 'quickly! Come with me – you will see something today that may help you in your new life. Quickly!'

In a trice we had the child in a hot bath. I issued instructions. Other treatment was given, and forty minutes later, a mother, with tears streaming down her face, took her baby into her arms, wrapped in a blanket. The danger was over. Perisi stood behind me.

'Bwana,' she said, 'there is a work of great satisfaction in the hospital here. That woman will listen to my words very greatly. Behold, does she not come from the village where Simba and I will live? Behold, there will be great joy when I can help people there in a way that they never thought was possible before.'

Perisi sat herself beside the woman on the steps of our hospital veranda and I saw them talking together. An hour later they were still talking.

At sundown when I walked through the hospital gates Perisi was waiting there for me.

'Bwana,' she said, 'behold, I have joy in my heart. That woman has said to me that when we start our hospital and our school, she will be one of those who help, even if it is only carrying water. She said that what she has seen today has come as great light; even as one walking in the darkness before the dawn rejoices when the sun comes up.'

'Perisi,' I said, 'how do you feel yourself? Have you recovered from your sickness? Is your strength what it used to be?'

'Bwana,' replied the African girl, 'there is sometimes weakness in my legs, but it is a small thing. Sometimes it feels as though there were ants crawling inside me where you sewed me up, but that, too, is a small thing. Behold, I have good strength.'

Three days went by, as they do in our hospital, hectically. Operations, scores of out-patients, injections by the hundred, and babies and babies and babies. It was about three o'clock in the afternoon. Suddenly I heard the big drum. I had a mask over my nose, on my hands were rubber gloves. The job I was doing would keep me going for the best part of an hour.

I turned to old Sechelela, '*Kah*, Sechie, and I was looking forward keenly to being at the wedding of Perisi and Simba this afternoon. *Kah!* This is a disappointment.'

As soon as I could I hurried down to the village on the side of the hill. When I arrived there, Daudi met me. He was the best man.

'Bwana,' he said, 'we waited till you came. Behold, both Perisi and Simba said they could not have this wedding until you were here. Did you not save both their lives, and behold, they want you to play the organ.'

Now a thousand and one African *dudus* and an assortment of rodents had not improved that organ. Nor was my technique particularly polished, but as I coaxed the well-known music of the 'Wedding March' out of the ancient musical instrument, I saw walking down the middle of that church, between crowded forms, my two African friends, who were on the threshold of life together.

Somehow I missed the first part of that wedding ceremony. My thoughts went wool-gathering over the last few months. I could see below the pale-pink shorts that Simba wore the scar where the lion had attacked him. There was a slight puckering beneath the eyes where my not-too-expert surgery had changed what would have meant early blindness into normal sight, and I felt the perspiration coming out on my brow again as I thought of those grim days when Perisi's life had been in the balance.

I became alive again to the present situation hurriedly as I heard Simba's deep voice replying to the African clergyman, '*Heeh – Vyo notendo*, Yes, I will,

and then the words in Chigogo repeated softly but firmly in Perisi's voice.

'Do you take this man as your wedded husband?'

In my mind I translated the Chigogo words into my home tongue:

'To live together in God's way, in the holy estate of marriage, will you obey, serve, love, honour and keep him in sickness and in health…'

There was the briefest pause. Perisi, a smile on her very comely face, looked at Simba, and he smiled back. Slowly and distinctly she said, 'I will.'

From Jungle Doctor Stings
a Scorpion

1

Mafununhula

'Peroxide,' said Daudi, 'and call the Bwana with feet that make dust fly. Tell him it's *mafununhula*.'

The message reached me in such dramatic form that I arrived at the hospital panting and out of breath.

'Daudi, what's this *ma-fun-un-hula?*'

'Nose-bleeding, Bwana, rather brisk, and the girl who's doing it all is Nzugu, the small daughter of Mubi, the Chief.'

He pointed to a tray. 'Everything's ready.'

Half a minute later, a rather scared small girl had a rolled-up piece of cotton-wool soaked in peroxide up her nose.

'Push with your finger against it, Nzugu, and the bleeding will stop. That's it. Pinch one side of your nose so that the cotton-wool comes right up against the place where the bleeding comes from.'

Rather gingerly she did so, and then found it didn't hurt. In a few moments the bleeding had stopped.

'What started it off, Nzugu?'

'Sneezing, Bwana,' and then, with a grin that was somewhat twisted by the cotton-wool up her nose, 'those of my household are experts in the matter of sneezing. *Heh*, my father – he sneezes with strength, but my sister Wendwa, *hongo!* Sneeze? Bwana!' She raised her eyebrows.

'Wendwa? – didn't she go to school here?'

'*Eh-heh*, Bwana, she still does, but these days she is visiting in my father's village.'

'Well, if she sneezes more strongly than you do, she'll get *mafununhula*, too!'

Daudi was putting everything in order on the tray again.

'Funny thing, I've never heard the word "*mafununhula*" before.'

My African assistant smiled.

'*Heh*, truly, say things like that, Bwana, and you will hear of it again.'

Carefully I removed the plug of cotton-wool from Nzugu's nose.

'*Yoh*, it's stopped, Bwana.'

'*Eh-heh*, that is good, but be careful how you sneeze in future. Here is some more cotton-wool and the medicine. I will leave it in this little dish beside your bed. You know what to do if it starts again?'

'*Eh-heh*, Bwana, I could do it.'

Daudi and I walked back to the hospital along the frangipani-lined track. Pedalling violently towards us was an African on a woebegone looking bicycle. He leapt off.

'Bwana, I come from Mubi, the Chief of the village of Iganha. Wendwa, his daughter – the strength has gone from her body. She has…'

'Yes,' said Daudi, 'we know – *mafununhula*, and the Waganga – the witch-doctors – have not helped her, *heh*?'

The messenger nodded.

'Bwana, the Chief is getting Suliman the Indian to bring her in to hospital in his lorry after nightfall.'

'Why after nightfall, Simba?'

He shrugged his broad shoulders. 'It's a matter of witchcraft. There are eyes to see and spells to be cast in the daylight.'

'They say her trouble is caused by a spell?' asked Daudi.

Simba nodded vigorously.

'She sneezes with strength. Is not this the cause of her *mafununhula*?'

'Let me know directly they arrive, Daudi. Get as much of her story as you can.'

The African assistant nodded. '*Ndio*, yes, Bwana.'

Two hours after sunset I heard running feet.

'Bwana,' came Daudi's voice, 'they've brought in Wendwa, Mubi's daughter. She's been nose-bleeding for nearly two days. I think she's dying; there's hardly any pulse. She breathes in little sighs, like someone very tired. Bwana, hurry, her nose still bleeds with strength.'

She lay on a blanket on the hospital verandah, surrounded by people. She was dangerously shocked.

Those with her moaned and swayed on their feet as they chanted a dirge.

'She will die,' they said mournfully.

I lifted her with Daudi's help and soon she was in bed. She was a girl of seventeen or so.

Marita, the nurse on nightduty, tucked in the blankets.

'What would you do in a case like this?'

'Treat shock and stop the haemorrhage, Bwana.'

I nodded. 'Marita – morphia, hot water bottles, blankets, get 'em ready. Daudi, boil up these instruments and get these dressings.' I scribbled a list.

Rapidly we worked. Outside, the relations talked in hoarse whispers.

Marita appeared with the morphia. I injected, and helped with the blankets and hot water bottles, then, borrowing the nurse's scissors, I snipped off charms from her wrists and neck.

'Witch-doctor's futility,' I thought, 'more use in a museum than a hospital.'

Daudi came hurrying in with a tray.

'Hold her head, Marita, while I pack the nostril with gauze.'

'*Ndio*, Bwana.'

'Take her pulse, Daudi.'

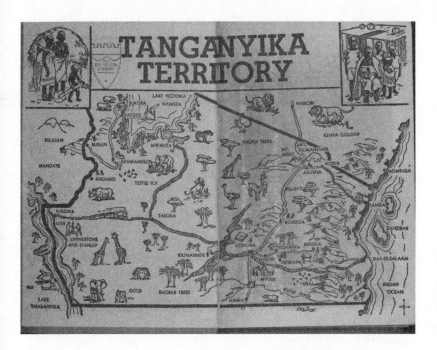

He went into the sterilising room and returned with an alarm clock. Solemnly grasping the large and dilapidated timepiece in one hand, Daudi felt the girl's pulse. As the second hand moved round to the minute, he grunted.

'Bwana, her pulse is over 200, and it is as soft as the small wind before dawn.'

'We're not on the right spot. Here, hold her head like so.'

I looked down her throat with a small torch and could see a trickle of blood.

'*Kah,*' Daudi's face was very concerned. 'Is there nothing we can do at all? Are we beaten in this?'

'Watch.'

169

Out came the gauze. Gently I pushed a very thin tube up her nostril.

'Hold that light, Daudi. I must see right in behind her tonsils.'

Slowly the tube was coaxed on until it appeared in her throat. I groped for long forceps and with them grasped the rubber, pulling it out of her mouth.

'*Hongo*, Bwana, it goes into her nose and comes of her mouth!'

'Truly, but watch.'

I rolled up gauze, stitching it firmly to the rubber and attaching a length of tape. Carefully we checked the firmness of the thread.

'See, Daudi, pull the tube, in goes the gauze right over the bleeding place, tape out here over the corner of her mouth. Keep it there with a bit of sticking-plaster and all should be well. The tape is to get out easily afterwards.'

Daudi rolled his eyes and made the whole range of African noises that express amazement.

Carefully we watched, but the bleeding had stopped. Wendwa's head was lowered.

'Haemorrhage controlled. Now to fight her loss of blood.'

'Fluids in every way possible,' said Marita.

'Carry on,' I smiled, and wrote in the Report Book: "9 p.m. Pharynx plugged; Shock treated; Morphia gr. ¼; Fluids; Pulse feeble 200."

The door opened and Sechelela came quietly in. From outside came a moaning dirge.

'Terrible row, Seche.'

She nodded. 'They think she will die. She…'

Then Wendwa sneezed seven times. Hastily the plug was readjusted. Marita looked at me with raised eyebrows.

I nodded.

'Drink this, Wendwa.'

The girl tried and then said, in a muffled voice:

'I can't swallow properly. There is a big thing in my throat. Also my head swims and spins.'

She drank again, spluttered and then sank back.

'I'll watch her till 10 p.m., Marita.'

The hands of the old alarm clock moved towards the hour. I dipped the pen in a bottle of ink and wrote on.

Suddenly a cockroach's head appeared through a crack in the door. I watched it come right out, then suddenly threw the pen like a spear. The insect fell to the floor. My foot came down on it smartly.

To my surprise, Wendwa's voice came weakly from the bed.

'You are a hunter of courage, Bwana.'

I grinned. 'What fun it would be to stop *mafununhula* in an elephant, Wendwa."

I loosened the tube and peered down her throat.

'Stopped.'

She drew in her breath sharply.

'I'm going to sneeze, Bwana. I'm going to…'

'No, you're not.' I put my finger firmly under her nose and pressed. 'What ever you do, O daughter of Mubi, don't sneeze.'

Her eyes twinkled. 'My father sneezes with strength,' she whispered.

'Does he? Well, don't follow his ways. Swallow this pill, it will stop your desire to do so. Sleep now, and, Marita, report any change to me at once.'

In the moonlight outside the ward were sitting a number of Wendwa's relatives, among them a picturesque old man with elaborate ear adornments and a native axe in his hand. He rose and greeted me.

'*Mbukwa*, Bwana.'

'*Mbukwa*,' I replied.

'I am her uncle, Bwana. Her father Mubi seeks news. Will she recover?'

'That, Great One, is in the hands of God. We have stopped the bleeding, but she is very weak. Much of her blood has been wasted.'

'*Kah,*' said the old man, 'and a cow and two tins of food were paid for spells to be made which would stop the bleeding.'

Behind him were three old African women. I turned round to them.

'Tell me, O wise ones of the tribe, what would you do if a small hole appeared in your water-carrying gourds?'

'*Yoh,*' said one old woman, 'we would plug it with a thorn or with cloth so that the water would not run out.'

'You answer with wisdom, but would you cast spells to close the hole or would you plug it?'

The old woman shook her head.

'Would you cast spells for a little thing like that?'

'Listen, then, to the news of Mubi's daughter. She had a little hole in a little vein, and I simply plugged it. There is no danger now from that. Wendwa, however, is not like a water-pot. You may refill one of these easily again with water at the well if it leaks, but how may you fill a body again with blood when much has leaked out?'

They shook their heads. 'It is an impossibility.'

'No, it is not an impossibility, but it will mean much work. But first, we will rest her and give her strength for whatever the future will hold.'

'Bwana,' said the old man, 'yours is the way of wisdom. Surely the hospital has great merit. *Assante sana*, thank you greatly.'

They turned and went away.

'Marita, call me if the pulse rate rises.'

Drums throbbed on through the night. At midnight Marita was outside the mosquito-proof wire of my window.

'Bwana, Bwana,' she called.

'*Nhawule*, what's up?'

'Wendwa's pulse races and flutters.'

'Be there in five minutes, Marita,' and I was.

The tube had moved. Wendwa's voice came softly.

'I sneezed, Bwana, and it started again. I'm frightened, everything goes round and round.'

'Hold on to me, it'll help, for I, too, often feel like that but I put my hand in His and fear goes.'

She gripped my arm while another plug went in.

173

'You mean Jesus,' she whispered.

'Yes, He knows just what to do whenever I'm in trouble.'

'Bwana, tell me about Him.'

'I will, but first, another injection.'

She hardly moved as the needle pierced her skin. I settled down on a stool beside her bed and started.

'One day there was a great one who had a daughter whose stay on earth had covered twelve harvests. She was greatly ill, and all her relations grieved for her with much wailing. But He came when they were *chengering*.'

On the night air faintly came again and again the *chenga* – the alarm signal of the tribe.

Marita looked up at me anxiously and whispered, 'Even now in the village the *washenzi*, the tribesmen, wail for someone who has died.'

Wendwa, heavy-eyed now, looked up. 'Bwana, go on.'

'Right. Well, He said to those who wailed, "She is not dead, she is asleep." They laughed with strength, but He took her by the hand and spoke words gently, and she sat up, fully alive again. You see, He was the Son of God.'

Wendwa lay back on her pillow.

'Bwana,' she whispered, 'I think He's here now.'

As we watched, her eyes closed, she relaxed and soon slept. The village drums throbbed still. I walked quietly to my house, knowing that the African girl was right – the Son of God Himself had been with us that night in Tanganyika.

Jungle Doctor Series

CHRISTIAN FOCUS PUBLICATIONS

Christian Focus | Christian Heritage | CF4K | Mentor

Christian Focus Publications publishes books for adults and children under its four main imprints: Christian Focus, CF4K, Mentor and Christian Heritage. Our books reflect that God's word is reliable and Jesus is the way to know him, and live for ever with him.

Our children's publication list includes a Sunday School curriculum that covers pre-school to early teens; puzzle and activity books. We also publish personal and family devotional titles, biographies and inspirational stories that children will love.

If you are looking for quality Bible teaching for children then we have an excellent range of Bible story and age specific theological books.

From pre-school to teenage fiction, we have it covered!

Find us at our web page:
www.christianfocus.com

CF4•K
Because you're never too young to know Jesus